City and Guilds of London Institute

A

Short History

1878-1992

Design and Typesetting by
Print Studio, City and Guilds

Published by
City and Guilds of London Institute 1993
76 Portland Place, London W1N 4AA

ISBN 0 85193 010 7

Cover illustration – New Headquarters, 1958 – from the Architect's drawing

Offset Litho Reproduction

Phototypeset in 10/14 Palatino and
printed on 130 gsm Fineblade Smooth

Printed in England

Contents

Foreword by John A Barnes, CBE, Director-General   ix

Introduction   11

Chapter 1   Foundation and Establishment, 1878-1889   21
Chapter 2   Unimpeded Growth, 1890-1918   46
Chapter 3   Government Constraints, 1919-1933   63
Chapter 4   Leadership in Technical Education, 1934-1943   78
Chapter 5   Growing Government Interest, 1944-1964   88
Chapter 6   Alignment with the State System, 1965-1992   115

Appendices

1   Institute Premises   165
2   The Visitors of the City and Guilds of London Institute   167
3   The Presidents of the Institute   168
4   The Vice-Presidents of the Institute   169
5   The Chairmen of Council   171
6   The Chairmen of the Executive Committee   172
7   The Joint Honorary Secretaries of the Institute   173
8   The Treasurers of the Institute   174
9   The Chairmen of the Examinations Committee   175
10   The Chief Officers of the Institute   176

Unpublished Sources   177

Bibliography   178

Index   180

Tables and graphs

Table 1 City and Guilds Technological Examinations 1879-1992:
Summary of Results   37

Table 2 Examination entries in industrial groupings 1892 and
1992 – also shown as charts   40

Table 3 Industrial groupings by size of examination entry
1892 and 1992   43

Table 4 Subjects and candidate entries 1892   44

Table 5 City and Guilds Staff numbers – also shown as a graph   162

Graphs of Candidate entries 1879-1992

Graph 1 1879-1934
Steady growth of candidate numbers to 1910 – then World War I and
recovery   77

Graph 2 1934-1964
Substantial growth in candidate numbers   87

Graph 3 1964-1992
Continuing major growth (from 1988 component entries have been
reported, rather than examination entries, following the adoption
of credit accumulation).   114

Illustrations

(between pages 96 and 97)

1 City and Guilds Certificate, 1886

2 City and Guilds Certificate, 1993

3 Mercers' Hall – the Institute's birthplace

4 Gresham College – the former Head Office

5 City and Guilds Finsbury Technical College, c. 1885

6 Mechanical Engineering Laboratory, Finsbury, c.1910

7 City and Guilds Central Institution, c.1885

8 Engineering Workshop, City and Guilds Central Technical College, c. 1910

9 Examination Centres of 1931 in England and Wales

10 Examination Centres of 1931 in Scotland

11 Examination Centres of 1931 in Ireland

12 HRH The Duke of Edinburgh laying the Foundation Stone of City and Guilds' Headquarters at 76 Portland Place, London, W1, 18 February 1958

13 City and Guilds Headquarters, 1958

14 Examination Papers in transit, 76 Portland Place Basement, May 1961

15 City and Guilds Gold Medal for Craft Excellence: Dr Graham White and The Rt Hon The Lord Mayor of London, Sir Hugh Bidwell, GBE, at Clothworkers' Hall, 8 March 1990

16 Information Technology students, 1991

Foreword

This *Short History* of the City and Guilds of London Institute is intended to give an account of the Institute and its work as a technical testing and examining body – those aspects of its Founders' initiatives that have continued essentially unchanged from 1878 to the present day. Less emphasis is given to the institutions and organisations created by City and Guilds – notably the Central Institution, Britain's first "industrial University", which became the City and Guilds College of the Imperial College of Science and Technology, University of London: the City and Guilds Finsbury Technical College, the prototype "college of further education": and the City and Guilds of London Art School for the practical arts which still flourishes as an independent trust.

The *Short History* therefore adopts a different standpoint from the two main published works which it seeks to supplement rather than to repeat – Jennifer Lang's *Historical Commentary,* and Adrian Whitworth's *City and Guilds College, 1885 – 1985.* Although there is very little published material on the Institute's history and activities, there is a wealth of unpublished sources. The City of London Guildhall Library Department of Manuscripts holds the Institute's Archives including copies of Minutes and annual Reports up to and including 1967; also Programmes of Technological Examinations up to and including 1939-40. The more recent records are held at the

Institute's Headquarters at 76, Portland Place, London W1. Documentary sources have been amplified by the reminiscences, particularly, of Sir David Woodbine Parish, CBE, and Mr Arthur Nutt. Sir David joined the Institute in 1953 as Representative of the Clothworkers' Company, served as Chairman of Council 1967-79, and is a Vice-President for life, appointed in 1979. Arthur Nutt joined the staff in 1927 as a Clerk in the Department of Technology and retired in 1974 as Head of the Examinations Department and an Assistant Director.

It is now timely to prepare this History to bring together the documentation into readable form. Advantage has been taken of the availability of Peter Stevens (a member of staff for 27 years and Secretary from 1989-91) on his retirement to research and compile it. This History is largely his work.

Others to be acknowledged for their help and support are Mrs Olive Foss, MBE a former Deputy Director of the Institute who has read and commented upon the manuscript, Mrs Linda Foreman, Miss Beverley Goss and Mrs Claire Gopoulos who produced the typescript, Mrs Elana Mellowes who did the typesetting, Mike Jones who prepared the cover artwork and Bruce Drew who prepared the diagrams.

It is quite rare to record in detail the history of examining bodies and their importance in sometimes shaping but always reflecting the trends and developments in education and training. This *Short History* of the City and Guilds of London Institute, a proud and independent part of the scene for 115 years, is designed to fill part of that gap.

J A BARNES
Director-General 1985-93

I n t r o d u c t i o n

Agreement to establish an Institute for the Advancement of Technical Education took the Corporation and Livery Companies of the City of London seven years to achieve. (Ironically, at the time, seven years was the traditional duration of apprenticeship, which the founders of the City and Guilds of London Institute saw their initiatives as superseding.)

Technical Education was one of the many great movements for popular improvement that ran through Victorian England. It arose in the growth of the factory system and as a consequence of the Industrial Revolution. In 1823 the London Mechanics' Institute was founded (it developed into Birkbeck College of the University of London): in the same year *The Mechanic's Magazine* started publication. Mechanics' Institutes were established in the main industrial centres throughout the country, the greatest numbers being in Lancashire and Yorkshire: altogether some 700 were established. Only slow progress could be made, mainly because of the defective primary education of many of the students – who were artisans studying in the evenings after a full day's work. An equal drawback was the unwillingness of the majority of employers and master craftsmen to reveal their technical methods to potential competitors. The Society for the Diffusion of Useful Knowledge, founded in 1826, was intended to supplement the work of the Mechanics' Institutes by publishing low-cost technical books and magazines.

11

Further support for the Mechanics' Institutes in and around Manchester was provided by the foundation in 1847 of the Union of Lancashire and Cheshire Institutes, Britain's first examining body in the field of technical education.

The application of science to industry was encouraged by the Great Industrial Exhibition in the Crystal Palace in Hyde Park in 1851; by the establishment of the Government Science and Art Department in 1853; and by the virtual re-foundation of the Society of Arts ("the Society for the Encouragement of Arts, Manufactures and Commerce") on its Centenary in 1854. Both the Science and Art Department and the Society of Arts introduced schemes of examinations to serve the Mechanics' Institutes.

In the City of London, the Clothworkers' Company from 1870 onwards gave substantial financial support to the Leeds Textile Industries School in Yorkshire; and other Livery Companies were supporting their original trades, or considering how they might become more closely associated with them under the changing conditions of industry.

The first concerted action by the Corporation and Livery Companies (the medieval "Guilds") of the City of London in connection with Technical Education was taken in response to a letter dated 24 November 1871 to the Lord Mayor from Thomas Hughes, MP, Chairman of the Crystal Palace Company, proposing the holding of exhibitions of industry for educational purposes. This was the Thomas Hughes (1822-96) who is now best known as the author of *Tom Brown's Schooldays*. He was a great social reformer and from 1854 was connected with the Working Men's College in Great Ormond Street, London and its Principal 1872-83. On 20 December 1871 the Lord Mayor issued a circular to all Masters and Prime Wardens, and the Upper Bailiff, of the Livery Companies, convening a meeting at the Mansion House to be held on 10 January 1872 "with the ultimate object of initiating a movement for the encouragement of Art, Manufacture, and Technical Education in connection with the City of London".

At the meeting it was resolved "That it is desirable that a Committee be appointed to represent the Corporation and the several Livery Companies to consider how Technical Education can be best promoted, such Committee to be presided over by the Rt Hon the Lord Mayor and to be composed as follows:-

viz.

The Lord Mayor and eleven members of the Corporation of London –	12
One member for each of the Livery Companies –	76
Total (members) –	88"

At a meeting of representatives of the Livery Companies at the Mansion House on 5 July 1872, views were expressed on education; apprentices; prizes; exhibitions; the freedom of the Companies; and the grouping of Companies according to analogy of trade. It was resolved to invite written suggestions from the Companies, including suggestions which might advance Technical Education by the direct action of the Companies.

At further meetings at the Mansion House on 29 July and 24 September 1872 the establishment of Lectureships at Gresham College was suggested, and it was agreed that premiums or prizes for artisans should be given to schools willing to provide education in Technical Art or Manufacture; that public exhibitions of articles manufactured by artisans should be held, with prizes "of considerable value"; that premiums should be offered for scientific construction; and that inducements should be offered to Masters and their Workmen to take apprentices.

These resolutions were negatived or adjourned *sine die* at a meeting on 21 October 1872.

Other courses of action were advocated at the next meeting on 18 February 1873 at which the chair was taken by the new Lord Mayor, Sir Sydney Waterlow. Sir Sydney proposed that there should be evening lectures on technological subjects at the Livery Halls, and that a fund should be formed "for founding a College and to develop Technical Education". In this fund was the germ of the Institute. The meeting went on to reject the report from the previous meeting, and to resolve to refer to a Sub-Committee the preparation of "a definite plan for the promotion of Technical Education by the Livery Companies", to be put before the Courts of the Companies "for their discussion, assent or adoption". Sir Sydney was appointed Chairman of the Sub-Committee and its members represented the Worshipful Companies of Stationers, Skinners, Coachmakers, Mercers, Painter-Stainers, Tallow Chandlers and Turners.

The Sub-Committee met on 18 February 1873 at the Mansion House to commission the gathering of information about schools in the Metropolis and about "what the Livery Companies are doing in the matter of Technical Education". On 29 July they met again to receive the results where the Livery Companies were concerned, under the headings:-

"A   Those which have or are about to take steps to promote Technical Education either directly or indirectly (19 named Companies)

B   Those which either cannot, or do not intend promoting Technical Education, or are considering the subject (26 named Companies)

C   Those not replying (25 named Companies including the now defunct Company of Long Bow String Makers)."

By invitation of the Lord Mayor, Mr Cole, CB, of the Science and Art Department (later to become Sir Henry Cole, commemorated in the Henry Cole Wing of the Victoria and Albert Museum) was present to link the work of the Sub-Committee with that of a Conference held the previous week, on 21 July 1873, convened by the Prince of Wales in his capacity as President of the Commissioners of the Exhibition of 1851.

At this Conference, held at Marlborough House, there were present the Prince of Wales, The Earl of Carnarvon (Chairman of the Commissioners' Board of Management), Sir William Anderson, KCB, the Rt Hon the Lord Mayor, and representatives of 23 named Livery Companies. Mr Henry Cole and Major-General Scott were in attendance. The conference was held "with the view of discussing how Technical Instruction might be promoted by the City Companies acting in concert with the International Exhibitions."

The Prince of Wales said he hoped the Companies would co-operate in the task "of promoting the study of Science and Art as allied to Productive Industry" (words to be echoed in the Institute's Royal Charter). Lord Carnarvon said it was a "question of the best means of diffusing technical instruction among the people". He went on to refer to the Commissioners' plans for annual international industrial exhibitions at South Kensington; to the Livery Companies' interest in education through their schools; and to national economic competitiveness. The Lord Mayor referred to the Companies' individual efforts in Technical Education, and said "much more important results could be obtained by union, and especially by a union promoted by His Royal Highness". A sympathetic resolution promising support was passed unanimously.

Henry Cole's representations to the Sub-Committee on 29 July 1873 were followed by a deputation to the meeting from "The Trades Guild of Learning for the Promotion of Technical and Higher Education among the Working Classes of the United Kingdom", whose object was "to teach workmen a better way to do their work". The deputation drew attention to the failure of the apprenticeship system and the difficulties of working people. The Livery Company representatives foresaw difficulties in funding the Guild as it proposed, for the establishment of "technical libraries, trade museums, annual examinations in technical performance for the class of apprentices – also technical instruction to supplement the deficiencies of elementary education".

The last record of the Sub-Committee's activity was on 28 October 1873, when it met to resolve that the Minutes of its meeting on 29 July, "having been approved, be reported to the General Committee to be held on this day". The end of Sir Sydney Waterlow's Mayoralty coincided with the cessation of activity. Sir Sydney, a staunch Liberal, may have stimulated W E Gladstone, out of office since 21 February 1874, to launch his challenge to the Livery Companies in a speech at Greenwich in November 1875, to take up once again, by way of technical education, the purpose for which they were founded – of developing the crafts and trades.

A further meeting of representatives of Livery Companies was held at the Mansion House on 3 July 1876, at which it was resolved "That it is desirable that the attention of the Livery Companies be directed to the promotion of education, not only in the metropolis, but throughout the country, and especially to technical education, with the view of educating young artisans and others in the scientific and artistic branches of their trades." At this meeting a Livery Companies' Provisional Committee was formed to undertake the necessary detailed planning: its Chairman was Lord Selborne, Master of the Mercers' Company 1876-77 and Lord Chancellor in Gladstone's Governments, and its Joint Honorary Secretaries were the Clerks of the Mercers', Drapers', and Clothworkers' Companies, John Watney, William Phillips Sawyer, and Owen Roberts – all subsequently knighted.

At the same time a number of the Great Twelve Companies formed their own committees for the advancement of education, and the Minor Companies considered the matter in their Courts. The Clothworkers' Company on 6 December 1876 issued a Memorandum for private circulation on "the necessity for the Guilds of London to combine in establishing in London itself, with affiliated branches for the local centres of the various trades and industries, in the suburbs and in the provinces generally . . . a City and Guilds' Industrial Institute or University. . ."

Early in 1877 a conference was held between the committees of the Mercers', Drapers', and Clothworkers' Companies, which expedited the work of the Provisional Committee. On 21 February a meeting in Drapers' Hall of representatives of nine Livery Companies passed a series of resolutions for joint action by the Corporation and Companies towards the foundation of an Institute. These resolutions were conveyed to the Livery Companies' General Committee, appointed at a meeting in Mercers' Hall on 7 June 1877 convened by a notice dated 28 May 1877 from Drapers' Hall signed by W Phillips Sawyer and Owen Roberts. This meeting appointed an Executive Committee "for the purpose of preparing a scheme for a National System of Technical Education", with Lord Selborne as Chairman and F J (later Sir Frederick) Bramwell of the Goldsmiths' Company as Deputy Chairman. The Executive Committee comprised representatives of the Corporation of London and the Mercers', Drapers', Fishmongers', Goldsmiths', Salters', Ironmongers', Clothworkers', Armourers' and Brasiers', Cordwainers' and Plaisterers' Companies.

The Corporation and Companies had by this time made specific promises of financial support totalling £11 582.10s.0d. towards the nascent Institute – Sir Sydney Waterlow's "fund". The Executive Committee decided that its first step should be to invite reports on the best ways of applying these contributions to the expansion and improvement of technical education. By letter of 28 July 1877 from Mercers' Hall, the three Joint Honorary Secretaries invited reports from six eminent figures:-

Sir William (later Lord) Armstrong, industrialist; Mr (later Sir) George Bartley, philanthropist; Lt Col (later Maj Gen Sir) John Donnelly, educationalist (Science and Art Department; Society of Arts); Captain (later Sir) Douglas Galton, scientist; Professor Thomas Huxley, scientist; Mr (later Sir) Henry Trueman Wood, administrator (Society of Arts).

By December 1877 all the reports had been received by the Executive Committee, which early in 1878 presented its own printed Report, entitled *Technical Education,* to "the General Committee of certain of the Livery Companies of London".

The main points of the Report were:

(a) the object of the Livery Companies was "the improvement of the technical knowledge of those engaged in the manufactures of this country, whether employed as workmen, managers or foremen or as principals"

(b) the approach should be to give "knowledge of the Scientific or Artistic principles upon which the particular manufacture may depend"; not "by teaching the workman to be more expert in his handicraft" – the latter improvement "must be derived from greater assiduity in the workshop, and from longer practice therein", and therefore "except in special cases, it would be unwise to establish any place for teaching the actual carrying out of the different trades"

(c) to proceed by steps, "and not to commence upon an extravagant scale . . . the plan should be so framed as to admit of gradual development"

(d) the means to be adopted should be a Central Institution and Local Trade Schools: the former in London," for more advanced instruction"

(e) the Central Institution would "supply competent Teachers for the Local Trade Schools, and . . . there would also go forth from it a supply of superior Workmen, Foremen, Managers and Principals of Manufactories"

(f) the Local Trade Schools should teach "the application of Science and Art to particular trades", to "Foremen, Workmen, Apprentices and others"

(g) the founding of Local Trade Schools should be entrusted to "residents in the localities where these schools are most needed", with further support from the Livery Companies if necessary: this process should start immediately

(h) Examinations would be periodically held in the Central Institution as well as in the Trade Schools, Prizes would be awarded, and "Certificates of merit would be issued in connection therewith."

In these points is set out the basis for all that the City and Guilds of London Institute has done between 1878 and the present.

The Report continued, to give further details of the Executive Committee's proposals for the instruction to be given at the Central Institution; the Professorships; the Institute's annual budget (of £20 000 initially, of which £3000 was appropriated to the Local Trade Schools; all to be provided by the Livery Companies). The Executive Committee also set out its proposals for a draft constitution for "The City and Guilds of London Institute for the Advancement of Technical Education". The government of the Institute should be vested in:

The President and Vice-Presidents (not exceeding 12) – all to be Liverymen

The Board of Governors (say 300), to meet at least annually

The Council (say 80), to meet quarterly

The Executive Committee (say 40) – frequency of meeting not stated, but practice following the Institute's foundation was to meet monthly: the Executive Committee to have power to appoint such sub-committees as might be necessary.

The principles of these provisions were adopted, were incorporated in the Institute's Royal Charter of 1900, and continue to apply.

The Executive Committee's Report having been circulated to the Livery Companies' General Committee, a meeting of the latter was convened for 11 November 1878 at Mercers' Hall. It was resolved by representatives of the Corporation of London and the Worshipful Companies of Mercers, Drapers, Fishmongers, Goldsmiths, Salters, Ironmongers, Clothworkers, Dyers, Leathersellers, Pewterers, Armourers and Brasiers, Carpenters, Cordwainers, Coopers, Plaisterers, and Needlemakers to establish The City and Guilds of London Institute for the Advancement of Technical Education. Lord Selborne was appointed Chairman of Council, and Mr Frederick Bramwell Chairman of the Executive Committee. The administration of the newly-founded Institute was provided by the three Joint Honorary Secretaries, and its offices were at Mercers' Hall, the Hall of the first Livery Company in precedence in the City of London.

Chapter 1

Foundation and Establishment, 1878-89

The Institute having been founded, the Executive Committee set to work with a will, to give effect to its proposals as soon as possible. Its activities attracted the participation of a large number of distinguished individuals from engineering, science, industry and the City and Livery Companies of London. There was a considerable common representation between the Society of Arts and the newly-founded Institute, and from the beginning relationships were close and cordial. Two of those whose reports to the Executive Committee led directly to the foundation of the Institute, Donnelly and Trueman Wood, were particularly closely involved in the Society of Arts; Trueman Wood as Assistant Secretary, and as Secretary 1879-1917. In 1879-80 he acted as Assistant to the Honorary Secretaries of the Institute in effecting the transfer of the administration of the Technological Examinations from the Society to the Institute. In the Institute's first formal constitution, the Memorandum and Articles of Association of 1880, provision was made for the Chairman of Council of the Society of Arts to be *ex officio* a Governor of the Institute. Sir Frederick Bramwell, Chairman of the Institute's Executive Committee, was elected as Chairman of the Society's Council 1881-82.

In the early years the Executive Committee met at least monthly and sometimes twice in a month, with the exception of August and September. Meetings were usually at Mercers' Hall; occasionally at Goldsmiths', Drapers', or Gresham College. Gresham College became the Institute's Headquarters, 1881-1957.

In accordance with the original Report, the Executive Committee appointed Sub-Committees for the detailed conduct of the Institute's business: the Sub-Committees' activities were subject to approval by the Executive Committee, which was the driving force of the Institute: the Council and Governors' functions were largely to give approval and confirmation. The Sub-Committees were:

A   For the Central Institution

B   Finance and Administration

C   City and Guilds of London Technical College, Finsbury; University College, and King's College

D   Technological Examinations, South London Technical Art School, Miscellaneous Grants, Metropolitan and Provincial Agencies.

The three Joint Honorary Secretaries acted as Secretaries to the Sub-Committees; John Watney to A and B, W P Sawyer to C, and Owen Roberts to D.

The Technological Examinations conducted by the Institute on 22 May 1879 were based on those set by the Society of Arts in the previous year. A total of 202 candidates, of whom 151 were successful, entered from 23 centres in 7 subjects:

Cotton Manufacture; Steel Manufacture; Gas Manufacture;
Wool Dyeing; Alkali Manufacture; Telegraphy; Qualitative Blowpipe Analysis.

Altogether, 16 subjects were offered, there being no candidates for:

Paper Manufacture; Silk Manufacture; Carriage Building; Pottery and Porcelain; Glass Manufacture; Cloth Manufacture; Silk Dyeing; Calico Bleaching; Photography.

In 1880 a total of 816 candidates, of whom 515 were successful, entered from 85 centres in 24 subjects. In 1881 there were 1563 candidates, of whom 985 were successful, from 115 centres in 28 subjects. Thereafter the statistics are shown in Table 1 and Graphs 1-3.

The examinations were held on a similar basis to those of the Government's Science and Art Department in theoretical sciences and humanities. In both systems grants were paid to teachers on the successful results of their students. (The Institute discontinued this practice after 1892.) The Institute's system made use of the Science and Art Department's examinations in that to qualify for the award of the City and Guilds Full Technological Certificate – the complete qualification for inclusion in the Institute's Register of Approved Teachers and for this purpose equivalent to a University Degree – the candidate had to gain Honours in the Institute's Final examination in technology and also to pass at the Elementary level in specified Science subjects examined by the Department.

The syllabuses published by the Institute were drawn up by the Examiners named at the head of each, and were in two parts:

I   the statement that "The Examination will include questions founded on such subjects as the following, but will not necessarily be confined to these subjects" – followed by 10-15 itemised statements of essential features of the technology concerned;

II   the titles of the 5-9 Science subjects in which passes were required for award of the Full Technological Certificate.

The Examiners were eminent either as scientists or proprietors of businesses using the technology in question. Of the 29 Examiners named for 1880, eight were included in *Who's Who,* five of them gaining knighthood. Two others, G N Hooper for Carriage Building and James Garrard for Goldsmiths' and Silversmiths' Work, bore names still prominent in their fields. The flexibility of Engineering at this time is illustrated by the Examiner for Telegraphy, W H Preece, originally a Civil Engineer, President of the Institution of Civil Engineers in 1898-99, and at the same time Engineer-in-Chief and Electrician to The Post Office.

The continuity of the Institute's Examiners, contributing to the consistency of standards, was remarkable. Of the Examiners for 1880, ten were still acting 15 years later as either Consultative or Acting Examiners. Of these, four were still in post as Consultative Examiners 23 years later, in 1918.

In the first few years, the Examiners effectively exercised complete authority over their subjects. With the growth and success of the Institute's Technological Examinations, the Executive Committee progressively appointed an Examinations Committee (later Technology Committee) and an Examinations Board to control the provision of subjects and the conduct of examinations.

For 1879-1880, the Institute would afford facilities for carrying out an examination in the published subjects wherever a class for instruction was formed and sufficient candidates presented themselves, provided that a Local Committee undertook to carry out the examination according to the rules. A Local Committee was the Committee of any Art or Science School under the Science and Art Department, or any School Board, or any Local Examination Board under the Society of Arts, or any Special Local Committee for Technological Examinations approved by the Committee of the Institute.

Examinations were offered at Honours grade for foremen, Advanced grade for journeymen, and Elementary grade for apprentices.

Certificates in Technology of the 1st or 2nd Class were awarded to successful candidates: Full Technological Certificates as described above, and Preliminary Certificates to those passing the Institute's examinations only – the latter were exchangeable for the Full Technological Certificate on subsequently passing in the stipulated Science subjects.

Entry was at the candidate's free choice although it was expected that candidates would normally be employed in a capacity to which the examination was relevant. There was no age limit. Entry was made to the Secretary of the nearest Local Committee, by whom the names were forwarded to the Institute's Central Office in London from which the necessary arrangements were made and co-ordinated.

Examination was by printed papers, to be answered in writing on paper specially provided by the Institute. Where Practical Examinations were set, as in Blowpipe Analysis, the Institute sent specimens to centres.

Local Secretaries had the duty of allocating candidates' numbers; handling the question papers; security; forwarding scripts to the Central Office for onward transmission to the Examiners; and receiving and distributing Certificates and Prizes. No application by candidates for these was necessary. Local Secretaries were paid a fee by the Institute of 1s per successful candidate from their centre.

The Local Committees must have at least five members including the Chairman and Secretary. No member or officer might be a candidate. The Committees' duties were to publicise the Institute's examination system by circulating the Institute's (free) published Programmes, by Posters, and by encouraging potential candidates; to superintend the examinations under instructions issued by the Institute to Local Secretaries; and to aid the formation and watch the progress of classes of instruction in Technology, to visit the classes, and to examine and sign the Register – kept on a form supplied by the Institute.

Grants to Teachers in 1879-1880 were payable only to teachers of Science or Art classes under the Science and Art Department or who had passed the Institute's Honours grade examination in the Technological subject concerned. For each successful candidate at any grade, £2 was payable for a 1st Class and £1 for a 2nd Class. Candidates must be certified by their employers to be actually engaged in the industry (or a closely allied industry) to which the examination referred.

Teachers "desirous of forming classes of instruction" were to apply to the Secretary of the City and Guilds of London Institute for the Advancement of Technical Education, Mercers' Hall, E.C. stating their qualifications. If approved, they would be granted registration: if not, no payment was required.

Grants to teachers were conditional on the candidate having received 20 lessons of a minimum of 1 hour in a *bona fide* Technological subject. Claims for grants were to be submitted on the Institute's prescribed Form, signed by the Chairman, two members, and the Secretary of the Local Committee, and supported by the Register (as above).

Candidates were encouraged to attain high standards in the examinations by the award of Prizes and Medals in each subject by the Institute. Provided that at least 85% of full marks was scored and a 1st Class Certificate gained, the following Prizes and Medals were awarded:

Honours grade	1st Prize	–	£5 and Silver Medal
	2nd Prize	–	£5 and Bronze Medal
	3rd Prize	–	Bronze Medal
Advanced grade	1st Prize	–	£3 and Silver Medal
	2nd Prize	–	£3 and Bronze Medal
	3rd Prize	–	Bronze Medal
Elementary grade	1st Prize	–	£2 and Silver Medal
	2nd Prize	–	£2 and Bronze Medal
	3rd Prize	–	Bronze Medal.

The early question papers covered all three grades and opened with Instructions as follow: "The Candidate must confine himself to one grade only, Elementary, Advanced or Honours, and must state at the top of his paper of answers which grade he has selected. He must not answer questions in more than one grade. He is permitted to attempt all or any of the questions in the paper selected, but a full and correct answer to an easy question will ensure a larger number of marks than an incomplete or inexact answer to a more difficult one.

In all cases the number of the question must be placed before the answer in the worked paper.

Three hours allowed for this paper.

Elementary – Questions 1-8
Advanced – 9-16
Honours – 17-24."

The successful growth of the Institute's Technological Examinations is shown not only by the growth in numbers of candidates, but by the growing numbers of names on the Institute's published List of Registered Teachers, as below:

1881 – 116
1885 – 467
1895 – 1093 (grouped by subject: some names occur more than once.)

The stage of development reached in the provision of technical education nationally in 1881 and 1882 is indicated by an analysis of the centres for the Institute's examinations, which were designated as follows:

	1881	1882
Total Centres	110	134
Mechanics' and Working Men's Institutes	25	21
Schools of Science and Art	9	20
Technical Colleges	7	9
Literary, Scientific, or Library Institutes	6	7
Institutes	5	9
Training College (Exeter)	1	1
Schools	25	23
Board Schools	11	11
National Schools	7	5

Individual Centres included:

Bolton Co-operative Society's Rooms; Bristol Trade and Mining School; Bury Athenaeum; Bury Co-operative Science Classes; Chester Natural Science Society's Rooms; Crook, Peases' West Miners' Institute; Dublin Railway Works, Inchicore; Dublin Royal College of Science; Dundee YMCA; Edinburgh Science and Art Museum; Esh Colliery Crook Miners' Institute; Falmouth Polytechnic Hall; Gosport, The Market House; Guildford Town Hall; Halifax, Crossley Orphanage; Hull Navigation Schools; Hull Royal Institution; Leeds Co-operative Hall (Holbeck); Lincoln, Newland Lecture Hall; London, Ellerslie House, Lewisham; London, Central Telegraph Office; Longton, The Court House; Macclesfield Useful Knowledge Society; Nottingham University College; Radcliffe Co-operative Science Classes; Runcorn Gas Works; Southborough Mission Room; Stockport Sunday School.

The effects of the Institute's Technological Examinations in stimulating the spread, and systematising the content, of courses of technical education throughout Britain in the early 1880s can be seen in various sources. In 1880 the Institute put its own affairs on a sound footing by completing and registering under the Companies Act, 1867, a Memorandum and Articles of Association, and by appointing a full-time Director and Secretary, Philip Magnus. Soon after his appointment Magnus made a visit to centres of industry and technical education in the North of England, as a result of which changes were made to the Institute's Programme of Technological Examinations. 3000 copies of the amended Programme were distributed.

An article in *The Times* of 18 October 1881 refers to the Institute's good work. Attention was drawn to the importance of increasing the supply of teachers, and to the co-operation of manufacturers in drawing up syllabuses.

The Council's second annual Report to the Governors, adopted on 13 March 1882, states with reference to the Technological Examinations that "a considerable and important impulse is being given to the Technical Instruction of apprentices, workmen and foremen in the manufacturing centres throughout the Kingdom." The term "Technical Instruction" is used in acknowledgement of the appointment in 1881 of the Royal Commission on Technical Instruction, referred to later in the Report and of which Magnus was an energetic member. The Report continues, to speak of "progress . . . in the erection of buildings in provincial towns in which technical instruction is now being given in connection with the Institute's Examinations . . . much is still left to be done." Of the Institute's Certificates the Report states that they are "to be regarded as diplomas of efficiency . . . a practical as well as a theoretical knowledge of the subjects . . . students have already obtained promotion in their employment in consequence of their having passed the Institute's Examinations."

This Report concluded by stating the Council's aim to see founded a Technical School for Girls, and to extend still further the system of Technological Examinations.

The Council's first Report, on the year ending 10 March 1880, had been concerned mainly with the Central Institution and the problem of finding a site for it. The "City Fathers" wanted it to be within the City of London and desirably adjacent to the City of London School, but no suitable site was available. The Prince of Wales, to whom Lord Selborne and Frederick Bramwell wrote on 11 February 1880, resolved the problem, in his capacity of President of Her Majesty's Commissioners for the Exhibition of 1851, by securing the lease of some four acres of the Commissioners' estate at South Kensington to the Institute, at a yearly peppercorn rent of One Shilling. In consequence, The Prince of Wales accepted the Presidency ("Presidentship" in the Council's second Report), and Selborne, Bramwell, and Sir Sydney Waterlow were appointed as Vice-Presidents of the Institute and as Commissioners for the Exhibition of 1851.

The third Report, for 1882, referred to the continued progress of the Institute and its increasing influence in promoting Technical Education. The value of the Technological Examinations in promoting sound technical instruction was "daily becoming more generally recognised both by employers and employed." The "system of annual examinations and payment on results" operated "side by side with those of the Science and Art Department", but, perhaps because of "the great difficulty in obtaining properly qualified teachers", of 1222 successful candidates only 450 qualified for the Full Technological Certificate (FTC) by having passed the Science and Art Department examinations.

The continuous development of the Institute's examinations since their introduction brought about the decision in 1882 that the published Programme would in future include for all subjects a suggested three-year curriculum, thus contributing to a progressive system of study.

By 1883, "the classes in connection with the Technological Examinations have in many instances developed into well-organised Technical Schools, to some of which the Council has provided pecuniary help."

The Institute's own examples of this process of development were the Finsbury Technical College and the South London School of Technical Art. In both cases the announcement that the Institute was "open for business" and had funds, contributed by the Livery Companies, available to support deserving ventures in technical education brought applications for grants to resuscitate classes that were otherwise in danger of expiring. The evening classes in the premises of the Cowper Street Middle Class School in Finsbury, and the Applied Art Extension of the Lambeth Art School, were adopted by the Institute for financial support and control. They developed respectively into the City and Guilds Finsbury Technical College, for which a special building was erected by the Institute, and the City and Guilds South London School of Technical Art, for which the leases of Nos. 122 and 124, Kennington Park Road were purchased – originally by Sir Sydney Waterlow personally, because the timetable could not wait for the necessary committee authority: the Institute indemnified him in due course.

Thus in the Institute's first year of existence its scheme of Technological Examinations and two of its three projected teaching establishments were in operation, and funds for the Central Institution were being accumulated from the Corporation and Livery Companies. Foundation stones were laid by members of the Royal Family in 1881, of Finsbury Technical College on 10 May by HRH The Duke of Albany (1853-1884, Queen Victoria's fourth son), and of the Central Institution at South Kensington on 18 July by HRH The Prince of Wales. As the Council's Report for 1881 states, Finsbury was "the first Technical College ever erected in London". Its completion and furnishing, and the preparation of its programmes of day and evening classes under the supervision of Philip Magnus acting as its first Principal, was the Council's preoccupation for 1882. At the request of the Corporation of London the City School of Art classes were transferred to Finsbury. By 1883, 100 day and 699 evening students had been registered. At the Central Institution the first handful of students – including one woman – were registered in 1884 and tuition started in earnest in 1885. The Art School began less spectacularly but equally effectively.

At the annual meeting of the Governors of the Institute on 19 March 1884 at Mercers' Hall, Lord Selborne said "We have arrived, I think, at a critical point of time in our Institution . . . at which I may congratulate you . . . upon the progress which things have hitherto made; but one at which it becomes necessary that we should proceed with renewed energies, if our great and useful undertaking is to go on prospering . . . Then I pass to the next and great branch of what I may call the Institute's own work – its Technological Examinations, by which it diffuses its influence and the power of its superintendence over the whole community throughout the United Kingdom. Nothing can be more striking, and nothing more satisfactory, than the progress of the work, and the testimony to its importance and usefulness which is shown in the Report (on the increase in numbers) . . . But what is still more remarkable, is the rapid extension of the desire to have the benefit of those examinations."

What is perhaps even more remarkable in 1992 is that the overall failure rate in the 1884 examinations was 49.7%. The Report stated that candidates "are already familiar with the practice of their trades, but possess a very imperfect knowledge of the application thereto of the principles of science."

The Report of the Royal Commission on Technical Instruction, published in 1884, endorsed the work of City and Guilds. Referring to City and Guilds Programmes of Technological Examinations, the Commissioners said "in view of the efficient and permanent working of these schemes, we should be glad to see the funds of the Institute made fully adequate to the efficient carrying out of the objects it has in view, which, in our opinion, is not yet the case."

The Institute's Report on its Technological Examinations for 1885 states: "The addition of practical tests to the written examinations previously held constitutes a new and important feature in the conduct of these Examinations. The Council are very desirous that these Examinations should serve the double purpose of improving the trades in connection with which the Examinations are held, and of affording a test which shall satisfy employers that the holders of the Institute's certificates are competent workmen; and at the same time practically acquainted with the scientific principles underlying the details of their trade."

In 1886 numbers continued to increase. The Board of Technical Education for New South Wales, Australia applied to enter candidates for the examinations of 1887. The Council reported "a very perceptible improvement in the character of the work sent up for examination", and their great satisfaction at the success of this department of their work, which it was their wish "still further to develop".

The standards of the Technological Examinations are indicated by the entry at Honours grade of students from King's and University Colleges, London; University College, Nottingham; and Firth College, Sheffield. Professor Graham, Head of Department of Chemical Technology, University College, London, wrote that he "finds the Institute's Examinations of great value in stimulating the work of the students."

The London School Board applied to the Institute in 1886 to co-operate in a scheme for handicraft classes for children attending Board Schools and others, and the Drapers' Company provided special funding of £1000 for this project. In 1888 Manual Training Classes in Elementary Schools were introduced jointly by the Board and the Institute. This provided the incentive for the Institute's provision for courses and certificates for Part-time Teachers of Handicrafts: the manual-training examinations were first held in 1892.

The Technological Examinations continued to gain momentum. The growing demand for City and Guilds' services, the volume of candidates (a total of 5508 in 1887), and the shortage of funds, all prompted changes. On the one hand there were increases in the amounts of grants on results, and further subjects were included in the Programme, for example Plumbing, in conjunction with the Plumbers' Company and the scheme for the national registration of plumbers. The assistance with the Technological Examinations of the Professors of the Central Institution was so great that from 1887 the administration of the examinations was "permanently to be carried on from the Central Institution." On the other hand, costs were rising. Notice was given of the discontinuation in 1888 of the Institute's provincial grants, the money being diverted to the growing needs of the Central Institution and Finsbury Technical College. The Council's Report for 1888 states that financial circumstances lead it to concentrate on "maintaining the efficiency of the Institute as a teaching body", and asserts the undesirability of "allowing it (the Institute) to be regarded as a mere instrument for the payment of money grants." The Council therefore looked to "wealthy provincial towns" to fund their own technical colleges and schools. Of the Technological Examinations: "The Council regret that the absence of sufficient funds has prevented them from adding to the subjects of examination or from further developing this branch of their work." Changes in the Regulations for the conduct of the examinations were made, to prevent too rapid an increase in costs, without discouraging attendance at classes. The Council "feel that the time has come for the localities to bear a larger share of the cost of conducting classes." The changes included the withdrawal of the Institute's money prizes: instead, Livery Company Prizes were introduced, where they could be obtained, in relevant subjects. The biggest change was the introduction of a nominal examination entry fee to candidates, "to prevent incompetent persons from presenting themselves", but too small "to discourage any candidate who values the Institute's Certificate from coming up for examination."

In introducing these changes, "the Council consider that the City and Guilds Institute may justly claim the credit of having given a notable impulse to the whole (Technical Instruction) movement, which, but for the action taken by the Corporation of London and the Associated Guilds twelve years ago, must probably have waited for the initiation of technical instruction by the State." (This statement harks back to Gladstone's speech of 1875: the Institute's subsequent development has been a process of interaction between it as an independent venture, and the State's initiatives.)

The first State initiative to affect the Institute was the Technical Instruction Act, 1889. The Act empowered local authorities to levy rates to aid technical or manual instruction in their localities: the distribution of the aid was to be controlled by technical instruction committees of the county borough councils (themselves recently formed). In consequence, the new councils began to provide technical instruction by way of both day and evening classes.

The immediate effect on the Institute was a proposal by a provincial branch of the National Association for the Promotion of Technical Education for the transfer of the conduct of City and Guilds' Technological Examinations to the Government. The opinion was expressed that the Act authorised the Science and Art Department of the Committee of Council on Education to include the Institute's technological subjects in its own system of examinations.

The Institute's Council responded to the proposal by seeking the opinions of all relevant sources so as to consider the question "with deliberation". They noted that "many of the leading manufacturing towns of the country have not exhibited that eagerness to avail themselves of the powers offered to them, which the promoters of the Act anticipated." The Council felt that "handing over to the Government a complete . . . branch of their operations, which has unquestionably attained much popularity and success, is a step not to be taken lightly." The outcome will be described in the following pages.

With specific reference to the provision of technical education in London, the State also intervened in 1889 in the shape of the Charity Commissioners and their scheme for the administration of the City Parochial Charities. Large sums were to be appropriated to the establishment and maintenance in London of Polytechnic Institutions. The Commissioners proposed to the Institute that the work of its Finsbury Technical College should be transferred to a new Polytechnic to be built in Northampton Square, Clerkenwell. The Institute's Council foresaw advantages from the scheme both in easing the costs and overcrowding of Finsbury, and increasing the pool of entrants to the Central Institution from all the new Polytechnics. The proposal foundered upon the Commissioners' inability to agree to fund the new Northampton Polytechnic to an amount at least equivalent to that invested by the Institute in the Finsbury Technical College. The Council held that the Institute was in a fiduciary position towards the Livery Companies which had provided the capital to build and equip its colleges, and could not therefore agree to close Finsbury on the terms proposed. It was however agreed between the Institute and the Charity Commissioners that the Institute would have representation on the newly-constituted City Parochial Foundation.

The first phase ends with the Institute founded and established in all its significant aspects, and coming into contact with initiatives by the State that will increasingly affect its future. Some of the "founding fathers" – Sir Frederick Bramwell included – have retired, and the first organising Director and Secretary, Sir Philip Magnus, has become Superintendent of Technological Examinations. In 1889 there was a total of 6606 candidates for the examinations.

Table 1 City and Guilds Technological Examinations 1879-1992: Summary of Results

Year	No of centres	No of subjects	No of candidates		No of passes	
1879	23	7	202		151	
1880	85	24	816		515	
1881	115	28	1563		895	
1882	147	37	1972		1222	
1883	154	37	2397		1498	
1884	164	43	3635		1829	
1885	167	42	3968		2168	
1886	192	48	4764		2627	
1887	216	48	5508		3090	
1888	240	49	6166		3510	
1889	231	46	6606		3532	
1890	219	49	6781		3507	
1891	245	53	7416		4099	
1892	265	55	8534		4469	
1893	288	55	9179		4847	
1894	346	54	9907		5481	
1895	353	58	10293		5824	
1896	380	58	10874		6263	
1897	406	62	11868		6720	
1898	369	63	13062		7553	
1899	397	63	14004		7962	
1900	390	64	14551		8114	
1901	380	66	14653		8143	
1902	364	66	15615		9155	
1903	396	65	16973		9860	
1904	419	66	19041		11293	
1905	440	69	19782		11838	
1906	444	69	20610		11665	
1907	439	69	21728		13054	
1908	443	72	22458		13058	
1909	404	73	23399		13665	
1910	418	75	24508		14105	
1911	465	75	24342		14206	
1912	447	75	22111		13886	
1913	448	74	21878		13618	
* 1914	467	73 (81)	23119 (24117)		14570	(15087)
1915	419	72 (78)	15623 (16287)		9866	(10215)
1916	316	71 (77)	8508 (8892)		5239	(5422)
1917	289	67 (72)	7508 (7832)		4514	(4635)

Year	No of centres	No of subjects	No of candidates		No of passes	
1918	296	63 (69)	7405 (	7656)	4723	(4860)
1919	312	65 (73)	8523 (	8791)	5221	(5382)
1920	321	67 (74)	9825 (	10664)	6231	(6779)
1921	316	67 (75)	7959 (	9179)	5369	(6204)
1922	319	72 (80)	9133 (	10274)	5772	(6503)
1923	320	74 (82)	8707 (	9724)	5924	(6737)
1924	297	73 (84)	8579 (	9634)	5602	(6350)
1925	299	73 (82)	8676 (	9973)	5738	(6563)
* 1926	332	81	11241		6638	
1927	354	85	11308		7051	
1928	375	84	12273		7853	
1929	395	86	13543		8673	
1930	402	86	14721		9616	
1931	425	93	15586		10388	
1932	423	95	15804		10579	
1933	421	97	16299		10693	
1934	425	101	17307		11430	
1935	433	108	18656		12084	
1936	445	115	20762		14050	
1937	470	118	24315		16765	
1938	501	120	29632		19894	
1939	556	125	34173		22000	
1940	427	116	15163		10515	
1941	439	108	12701		8780	
1942	495	110	16970		11224	
1943	673	104	20415		13261	
1944	790	113	24464		15057	
1945	1020	113	27322		16387	
1946	925	123	30889		18612	
1947	960	138	41323		26531	
1948	1010	152	52172		33655	
1949	1025	165	61513		38963	
1950	890	171	66679		43218	
1951	895	178	67780		42276	
1952	900	184	69337		43266	
1953	910	190	73990		46496	
1954	941	203	80685 (	89211)	48904	(53194)
ƒ1955 (1954-55)	967	217	87297 (	96875)	54087	(59253)
1956 (1955-56)	1010	232	96007 (	105895)	60765	(65805)
†1957 (1956-57)	1066	240	108771 (	119948)	67960	(73513)
1958 (et seq)			128814 (Total)		77121 (Total)	
‡1959			138476		82763	

Year	No of centres	No of subjects	No of candidates	No of passes	
1960			143661	85698	
1961			151882	91196	
1962			169289	101475	
1963			200241	117216	
1964			225186	141874	
1965			251221	161842	
1966			280995	183303	
1967			311643	206805	
ƒ1967-68 (Computer processed)			323563	232281	
1968-69			359064 (356780)	258756	
1969-70			373762	**Failed**	103636
1970-71			376443 (377828)		100876
1971-72			386861		102938
1972-73			397911		110450
1973-74			386718		107908
1974-75			395483		109691
1975-76			429814	**Awards**	113951
1976-77			445306 (450675)	314235	133560
1977-78			454608	316923	137685
1978-79			455634	318994	136640
1979-80			455836 (461303)	321479	134357
1980-81			473214 Awards made	333028	
1981-82			513223	345133	
1982-83	1795		527960	365131	
1983-84	2246		561171	400104	
1984-85			561841	369805	
1985-86			562426	377647	
1986-87			558884	414691	
1987-88			555513	381516	
1988-89 Total entries			1305633		
1989-90			1331410		
1990-91			1429056		
1991-92			2335005		

* Figures in brackets taken from Department of Technology Report, 1926 and include Overseas, Teachers' Certificates, and Special Examinations candidates: 1926 onwards grand totals given.

ƒ Presentation of statistics changed: brackets show Totals Home and Overseas.

† Presentation of statistics changed: brackets show Totals Home and Overseas.

‡ Home and Overseas Results published separately for first time: Totals shown above.

Table 2 Examination entries in industrial groupings 1892 and 1992

	1892		1992	
Extractive Industries	90	(1.5%)	293	(0.01%)
Process Industries	358	(4%)	53993	(2.3%)
Production and Maintenance Engineering	1221	(14%)	145530	(6.2%)
Electrical, Electronic and Informatics Engineering	689	(8%)	193841	(8.3%)
Vehicle and Plant Maintenance	212	(3%)	247189	(10.6%)
Textile, Clothing, Footwear and Leather	3650	(43%)	7137	(0.3%)
Construction and Construction Services	1929	(23%)	220303	(9.4%)
Media and Communication Industries	256	(3%)	9582	(0.4%)
Creative Arts, Crafts and Leisure Pursuits	29	(0.5%)	20688	(0.9%)
Agriculture and Allied			82400	(3.5%)
Furniture and Furnishing			12340	(0.5%)
Hotel, Catering, Travel and Recreation			152827	(6.5%)
Personal Services (Hairdressing, Health Education)			369790	(15.8%)
Retail, Wholesale, Distribution			157408	(6.7%)
Business and Commerce			41343	(1.8%)
Services to Industry and Commerce			120838	(5.2%)
Utilities			3522	(0.2%)
General Education and Work Preparation			424698	(18.2%)
Special Services			19250	(0.8%)
HM Forces			17346	(0.7%)
Joint City and Guilds/Foras Aiseanna Saothair			7497	(0.3%)
Senior Awards			2168	(0.1%)
National Examining Board for Supervisory Management			25022	(1.1%)
Totals	**8534**	(100%)	**2335 005**	(100%)

Examination entries in industrial groupings 1892

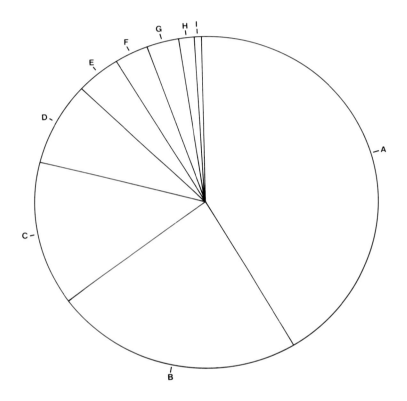

Key

A	Textile, Clothing, Footwear and Leather	3650	(43.0%)
B	Construction and Construction Services	1929	(23.0%)
C	Production and Maintenance Engineering	1221	(14.0%)
D	Electrical, Electronic and Informatics Engineering	689	(8.0%)
E	Process Industries	358	(4.0%)
F	Media and Communication Industries	256	(3.0%)
G	Vehicle and Plant Maintenance	212	(3.0%)
H	Extractive Industries	90	(1.5%)
I	Creative Arts, Crafts and Leisure Pursuits	29	(0.5%)

Examination entries in industrial groupings 1992

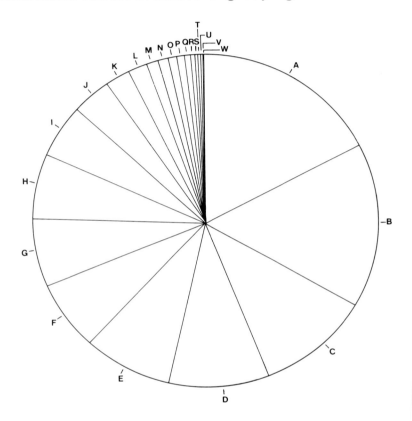

Key

A	General Education and Work Preparation	424698	(18.2%)	**L**	Business and Commerce	41343	(1.8%)
B	Personal Services (Hairdressing, Health Education)	369790	(15.8%)	**M**	National Examining Board for Supervisory Management	25022	(1.1%)
C	Vehicle and Plant Maintenance	247189	(10.6%)	**N**	Creative Arts, Crafts and Leisure Pursuits	20688	(0.9%)
D	Construction and Construction Services	220303	(9.4%)	**O**	Special Services	19250	(0.8%)
E	Electrical, Electronic and Informatics Engineering	193841	(8.3%)	**P**	HM Forces	17346	(0.7%)
				Q	Furniture and Furnishing	12340	(0.5%)
F	Retail, Wholesale, Distribution	157408	(6.7%)	**R**	Media and Communication Industries	9582	(0.4%)
G	Hotel, Catering, Travel and Recreation	152827	(6.5%)	**S**	Textile, Clothing, Footwear and Leather	7137	(0.3%)
H	Production and Maintenance Engineering	145530	(6.2%)	**T**	Joint City and Guilds/Foras Aiseanna Saothair	7497	(0.3%)
I	Services to Industry and Commerce	120838	(5.2%)	**U**	Utilities	3522	(0.2%)
J	Agriculture and Allied	82400	(3.5%)	**V**	Senior Awards	2168	(0.1%)
K	Process Industries	53993	(2.3%)	**W**	Extractive Industries	293	(0.01%)

Table 3 Industrial groupings by size of examination entry, 1892 and 1992

1892 (position in 1992 in brackets)   %
1	Textile, Clothing, Footwear, Leather (19)	43
2	Construction and Construction Services (4)	23
3	Production and Maintenance Engineering (8)	14
4	Electrical, Electronic and Informatics Engineering (5)	8
5	Process Industries (11)	4
6	Vehicle and Plant Maintenance (3)	3
7	Media and Communication Industries (18)	3
8	Extractive Industries (23)	1.5
9	Creative Arts, Crafts and Leisure Pursuits (14)	0.5

1992 (position in 1892 in brackets)
1	General Education and Work Preparation	18.2
2	Personal Services (Hairdressing etc, Health etc, Education etc)	15.8
3	Vehicle and Plant Maintenance (6)	10.6
4	Construction and Construction Services (2)	9.4
5	Electrical, Electronic and Informatics Engineering (4)	8.3
6	Retail, Wholesale, Distribution	6.7
7	Hotel, Catering, Travel, Recreation	6.5
8	Production and Maintenance Engineering (3)	6.2
9	Services to Industry and Commerce	5.2
10	Agriculture and Allied	3.5
11	Process Industries (5)	2.3
12	Business and Commerce	1.8
13	National Examining Board for Supervisory Management	1.1
14	Creative Arts, Crafts and Leisure Pursuits (9)	0.9
15	Special Services	0.8
16	HM Forces	0.7
17	Furniture and Furnishing	0.5
18	Media and Communication Industries (7)	0.4
19	Textile, Clothing, Footwear and Leather (1)	0.3
20	Joint City and Guilds/Foras Aiseanna Saothair	0.3
21	Utilities	0.2
22	Senior Awards	0.1
23	Extractive Industries (8)	0.01

Table 4 Subjects and candidate entries 1892

	Subject	Number of candidates' papers in 1892
1	Salt Manufacture	
2	Alkali Manufacture	
3	Soap Manufacture	6
4	Bread-making	13
5	Brewing	40
6	Spirit Manufacture	1
7	Coal-Tar Products	17
8	Sugar Manufacture	
9	Fuel	16
10	Painters' Colours, Oils, etc	22
11	Oils, Fats, etc	4
12	Gas Manufacture	54
13	Iron and Steel Manufacture	117
14	Paper Manufacture	10
15	Photography	71
16	Pottery and Porcelain	29
17	Glass Manufacture	
18	Dressing of Skins	
19	Leather Tanning	23
20	Boot and Shoe Manufacture	175
21	Silk Dyeing	
22	Wool Dyeing	119
23	Cotton Dyeing	65
24	Cotton and Linen Bleaching	50
25	Calico and Linen Printing	18
26	Wool and Worsted Spinning	118
27	Cloth Weaving	694
28	Cotton Spinning	1203
29	Cotton Weaving	878
30	Flax Spinning	10
31	Linen Weaving	29
32	Silk Throwing and Spinning	13
33	Silk Weaving	14
34	Jute Spinning	105
35	Jute Weaving	84
36	Lace Manufacture	4
37	Frame-work Knitting and Hosiery	43
38	Hat Manufacture	5
39	Telegraphy and Telephony	209
40	Electric Lighting	447

Table 4 Subjects and candidate entries 1892 (contd)

Subject	Number of candidates' papers in 1892
41 Electro-Metallurgy	33
42 Metal Plate Work	46
43 Plumbers' Work	825
44 Silversmiths' Work	
45 Goldsmiths' Work	29
46 Watch and Clock Making	63
47 Woodworking Tools	14
48 Metal-working	132
49 Mechanical Engineering	966
50 Road Carriage Building	127
51 Rail Carriage Building	69
52 Typography	189
53 Lithography	67
54 Ores, Raising and Preparation of	59
55 Mine Surveying	31
56 Milling (Flour Manufacture)	58
57 Carpentry and Joinery	886
58 Ship Carpentry	10
59 Ship Joinery	6
60 Brickwork and Masonry	215
61 Plasterers' Work	3
Totals, 1892	**8534**
Totals, 1891	**7416**

Chapter 2

Unimpeded Growth, 1890-1918

"The enactments of the Technical Instruction Act, 1889, and the subsequent provisions in the Local Taxation Act, 1890, by which Local Authorities in counties and in the larger municipalities have had placed at their disposal for the promotion of technical education large sums of money arising from licensing sales of wine and spirits, have changed the circumstances under which the City and Guilds Technical Institute organised their system of Technological Examinations, and of payment on results of examinations throughout the United Kingdom". So begins a *Memorandum on the Position of the Technological Examinations and Classes of the City and Guilds of London Institute to Local Authorities under the Technical Instruction Act*, by William Bousfield, Vice-Chairman of the Examinations Committee, issued on 8 January 1891. The main change was the discontinuation after 1892 of the payment by the Institute of grants on results. It was hoped that Local Authorities would themselves more than make up the loss of these grants from their new resources, and in most cases this is what happened. The Memorandum went on to describe City and Guilds' services to technical education and to make the case for it as the single examining body: "The alternative of a number of examining bodies scattered through the United Kingdom would not be as satisfactory as the development of the uniform system of the Institute. Such isolated examining bodies would inevitably lead to overlapping and to diverse standards of excellence in Certificates . . . We must recognise that . . . the examinations should be adapted to local wants by preparation of an alternative syllabus of instruction in these cases."

On 28 February 1891 the substance of this Memorandum was reissued over the names of the Chairmen of Executive Committee and Examinations Committee, and the Honorary Secretary to the Institute. It included the offer, without commitment, of the additional service of "the Inspection of classes by competent experts"; also of a system of reporting to County and Borough Councils on the attendance of students which, in conjunction with their examination results, could form a basis for the payment by local authorities of grants for the maintenance of classes, either as capitation grants or grants on examination success. Without such grants, the Institute feared that the Technological and Trade classes established over the past 12 years would be unable to continue to exist.

Fortunately by the next year the Council's annual Report is able to state: "The allocation of funds under the Local Taxation Act to technical instruction by County and Borough Councils has had the effect of largely increasing the number of technical classes, and of the students in attendance . . . It is believed that the withdrawal of grants on results by the Institute will not seriously affect the success of these classes which have for the most part been taken over or subsidised by the County Councils, and it is also believed that the Institute will retain its connection with the technical classes throughout the country, and that better educational results will be obtained." These beliefs turned out to be justified. In the London area the system of grants on results was retained for the time being, in response to the London County Council's decision to devote £90 000 to Technical and Secondary Instruction in the session 1893-94. The offer of Inspection of classes by the Institute was implemented in 1892 at the Municipal Technical School, Birmingham, and the Merchant Venturers' School, Bristol, stimulated by a special grant for this purpose from the Clothworkers' Company.

The Institute's Report on the Technological Examinations of 1892 states: "The Statistics . . . afford gratifying evidence that the popularity of the Examinations is each year increasing; but what is more important is the knowledge that the value of the Institute's Certificates is more generally appreciated by artisans and by employers, and that the Examinations are utilised by County Councils as a satisfactory means of testing the efficiency of the Technical Classes under their control." The theme of service to local authorities is further developed in the Report for 1893, which refers to the growing proportion of candidates gaining Internal Certificates (as having followed an approved course of study) rather than External; to the extension of Practical Examinations; to the introduction of the Teachers' Certificate in Metalwork to complement that in Woodwork; and to the increasing availability of specialisation in the questions set. "By ascertaining the opinion of teachers and seeking their help and advice in the conduct of the examinations, the Institute has been enabled to exercise an increasingly useful influence upon the teaching given in the Technical Classes in different parts of the country."

The second phase of the development of City and Guilds' Technological Examinations, essentially one of unimpeded (if slow and steady) growth, is characterised by a concern to establish improvements in teaching through co-operation with teachers. The special detailed reports which the Institute issued at this time "are intended to inform teachers and local committees . . . and to explain, in certain cases, the causes of the failure of the students of particular classes, and to direct attention to possible improvements in the methods of teaching."

The Technological Examinations of 1895 were entered by more than ten thousand candidates for the first time (a total of 10 293), and in addition to the United Kingdom were held overseas in New South Wales; New Zealand; and Bombay. The introduction of Preliminary examinations improved the Pass Rate at Ordinary Grade, but the work at Honours Grade was less satisfactory, and the attention of the Technical Education Committees of County Councils was "directed to the urgency of the need for the provision of advanced courses of instruction." In this and subsequent years an exhibition of candidates' practical work was held at the Imperial Institute in South Kensington, London (adjacent to the City and Guilds Central Technical College, as the Central Institution was re-named in 1893). A large increase in the Institute's work in the Inspection of classes was reported, with Inspectors of Boot and Shoe, and Textile, classes being funded by the Cordwainers' and Clothworkers' Companies. In the next year, 1896, it was reported that a total of 218 classes had been visited.

The object of the Institute's Department of Technology, by which the examinations were administered, was at this time stated to be "not so much the examination of candidates as the organisation and direction of technical teaching adapted to the requirements of artisans." The Preliminary examinations continued to give satisfaction, and were adopted in place of the Science and Art Department examinations to qualify for the award of FTC (the proportion of candidates passing the Science and Art Department examinations was "still very small"). The Council reported that its efforts to arrange courses of technical instruction for girls "have proved eminently satisfactory."

By 1896-97 reference was still being made to the difficulty arising from the absence of adequate preparatory training on the part of students attending Technological Classes, and to the time elapsing between leaving elementary schools and entering such classes. The pattern of many succeeding years' activities is set (allowing for the Victorian language) in the following passage from the Report on the work of the Institute's Technological Examinations Department of 1896-97:

"To several of the trade societies, now interesting themselves in Technical Education, the Institute is indebted for valuable assistance and co-operation; and although further encouragement of the educational work in which it is engaged may be expected from manufacturers and employers, there are indications of a fuller recognition on their part of the advantages which trade and industry derive from the better education of the operatives they employ. It is the constant endeavour of the Institute to adapt its schemes of instruction to local needs and to the changing requirements of different trades, and to make its examinations a true test of the technical knowledge and ability of the artisan students who have been trained in its registered classes. To this end, frequent changes are made in its syllabuses of instruction, and tests of workmanship, wherever practicable, are made a part of the examination. The difficulty of obtaining competent examiners increases year by year, and in many subjects this difficulty has to be met by the employment of more than one examiner and of assistant examiners conversant with different branches of the trade or manufacture."

This Report also announces the achievement during the year of agreements – with the General Post Office Telegraphic Department for a double salary increment to be given to Telegraphists holding the Institute's technological certificate in Telegraphy and Telephony, and with the Union of Lancashire and Cheshire Institutes to accept the ULCI Preliminary Textile examination for entry to classes in Spinning and Weaving. "The (Institute's) Committee feel that for the better organisation of technical education, every effort should be made to avoid the duplication of examinations, and of Examining Authorities, . . . " Practical examinations continued to expand: in this year the practical in Brickwork and Masonry was extended, and a practical test in Painting and Decorating introduced. Overseas, Pietermaritzberg, South Africa, and Jamaica had joined the list of centres.

In 1899 the Institute's Executive Committee accepted the invitation of the Commissioners for the University of London that the City and Guilds Central Technical College become a School of the University: the first (and at the time the only) School in the Faculty of Engineering. Of even greater long-term importance for the future of the Institute was the passing in this year of the Board of Education Act, by which a single Government Department became responsible for the powers and duties previously exercised separately by the Education Department and the Science and Art Department; and, in respect of education, by the Charity Commissioners. The powers of the new Board were extended to Secondary Education and to the Registration of Teachers. The Board included within its scope "matters relating to technical education." The power of inspection, withdrawn from the Institute in the Bill by the House of Lords, was reinstated by the Government on Third Reading. The Act created a Consultative Committee of the Board of Education. One of the duties of the Committee was to be framing regulations to govern the registration of teachers: while in the debate in the House of Commons Sir John Gorst said for the Government "in a question like technology, for example, the admirable instruction given by the City and Guilds Institute would be available".

This was a time when the Institute was riding high. Opening the annual exhibition of candidates' practical work at the Imperial Institute in June, the Lord President of the Council, the Duke of Devonshire, said "this Institute . . . have been, I think, the pioneers in the great work, which has subsequently been taken up by the Government, by Parliament, by the County Councils, by the County Borough Councils, and by other local authorities throughout the United Kingdom."

The grant to the Institute of a Royal Charter of Incorporation on 26 October 1900 denoted its acceptance as a recognised part of the constitution and national life of the United Kingdom.

One example of City and Guilds' contribution at the forefront of the technology of the day was the early military use of Wireless in the South African War. *The Times* reported that "most, if not all, of the assistants in charge of Marconi's apparatus . . . are men from the Finsbury and Central Colleges."

At Finsbury, however, the first signs of a threat to the viability of the evening Trade classes from the availability of similar classes in Bricklaying,

Carpentry and Joinery, Plumbing, Builders' Quantities, and Metal Plate Work at the various London Polytechnics were appearing, and the Institute began to consider transferring this aspect of its work at Finsbury to the responsibility of the London County Council Technical Education Board at its Hoxton Institute.

In establishing working relations with the new Board of Education, a deputation from the Institute to the Secretary of the Board, Robert Morant, pointed out the desirability of co-ordinating the work of the Institute's Technological Examinations Department with that of the proposed branch of the Board dealing with Technology. A joint Departmental Committee was appointed, which it was hoped would avoid the overlapping of examinations and would bring the instruction provided by County Councils and Technical Schools into a closer relationship with the Board of Education and the Institute. The Institute also made representations to the Lord President of the Council, in an effort to gain State aid for the teaching of Technology on the same basis as that of Science and Art.

To secure its place in the appointment of technical teachers, the Institute in 1900 revised its list of Teachers of Technology: the Register was published in the Programme for 1900. This Programme was published earlier than previous issues, the Calendar of Examination Dates having been co-ordinated with the Board of Education and the Science and Art Department, and additions and alterations to the Programme made at the request of the Association of Technical Institutions.

A most important development first reported in 1900 was the action taken by the Institute to encourage the formation of Advisory Committees, consisting of manufacturers and others, to advise on courses of instruction and examinations. The Council acknowledged especially the assistance received from Conferences with representatives of several trade organisations.

The Institute's Department of Technological Examinations' exhibit on the organisation of the examinations and examples of candidates' work at the International Exhibition of 1900 in Paris received the Grand Prix from the International Jury. Sir Philip Magnus wrote: "This award will no doubt be regarded by the Corporation and the Contributing Livery Companies as a very satisfactory recognition of their efforts to establish in this country a well-organised system of Technological Instruction applicable to all parts of the Empire."

In 1901 the City and Guilds' Central Technical College's foremost position among Engineering Colleges was recognised by the University of London in its offer to the Institute of a grant for the College of £1425 per annum, out of the grant to the University by the London County Council Technical Education Board to improve and extend the teaching of Engineering in the Metropolis.

Close relationships between the Board of Education and the Institute's Department of Technology developed over the arrangements published in the Board's *Directory* for approving "grouped courses of instruction in Technological subjects." Contacts were also developed with the Scotch *(sic)* Education Department and (in those pre-partition days) the Department of Technical Instruction and Agriculture in Ireland.

The Education Act of 1902 constituted the County and Borough Councils the Education Authorities for their areas, with extended powers and responsibilities. Changes in the conditions governing the award of Parliamentary grant to Local Education Authorities were made, so as to encourage the expansion of technical education. The recognition of technical education was prescribed by the Board of Education in the Codes of Regulations which it issued, from now on, regarding grant payments. These Regulations, periodically issued, effectively determined the structure of technical education within which the Institute would operate in future.

These changing circumstances were very fully considered in the Council's Report for 1902, and the Institute's future needs to fund its further expansion outlined. It was reported that "the certificates granted by the Institute, where they show that the candidates have passed certain examinations of the Board of Education in Science or Art subjects, are stamped as 'Issued under conditions approved by the Board'. . . . The Council welcome the attendance at the meetings of their Examinations Board of the four additional members appointed by the Board of Education, two of whom are officers of the Board, whilst the remaining two represent respectively the Association of Technical Institutes and the Association of Organising Secretaries, thus bringing the Institute into close touch with the Technical Schools and with the Local Education Authorities of the country . . . The Council take this opportunity of thanking the several Trade Societies for the encouragement they have given to apprentices and others to attend regularly technical classes . . . , and for the valuable prizes which they offer to those who succeed in passing the Institute's Examinations. The Department (of Technology) necessarily holds a sort of intermediate position between the educational and trade interests of the country, and it is the constant endeavour of the Institute to indicate by the schemes of instruction published in the Programme the intimate relation that should subsist between Workshop Practice and the teaching of Science and Art as bearing on trade processes, as well as on Engineering and Manufacturing operations."

The *quid pro quo* for the development of cordial and constructive relations between the Board of Education and the Institute was that "in all cases where important alterations are proposed, the syllabuses in Technology and in Manual Training shall be submitted to the Board, before being published in the Programme." One of the benefits was the Board's statement in its *Supplementary Regulations for Secondary Day Schools and for Evening Schools*, issued in July 1902, that "The following organisations have been recognised by the Board as agencies to conduct Inspections under the Act (of 1899) . . .

(1) University of Oxford
(2) University of Cambridge
(3) Victoria University (Manchester)
(4) City and Guilds of London Institute (in Technological subjects, Manual Instruction and Domestic Economy only)."

From 1 May 1904 the Education Act 1902 was applied by Parliament also to London, and the School Board for London and the Technical Education Board of the London County Council were replaced by the new LCC Education Committee. While this affected the Institute's Central Technical College, Finsbury Technical College, and South London School of Technical Art, the effects for the moment were more constitutional than practical.

The appointment of the Board of Education as a Government Department to concern itself with work in which the Institute had been taking the lead for some 25 years was bound to cause some problems, as was hinted in *The Times* of 12 June 1903, reporting the speech of the Board's President, Lord Londonderry, when opening the Institute's Exhibition of Students' Practical Work: "The community owed a great debt of gratitude to the (City and Guilds) Department of Technology, which had rendered a great service not only to London but to the country at large, for it had afforded for years the only guidance to local efforts which was available for our great industries; and by their action and generosity they had promoted the textile trade; the engineering trade; and industries of all sorts and kinds . . . His own Department had also in its special line done a great work. Their lines had to a certain extent been different; and therefore the two bodies, important and necessary as they were, and working for the same end, had been divided by a small gulf. He hoped to see that gulf bridged over and both branches of Technical Education, which were so necessary for the welfare of the country and its industries, welded together." The different lines referred to are taken to be the Board's approach through local initiatives by way of the control of finance, and the Institute's approach through national standards by way of the control of content. ("He who pays the piper . . . ").

The support of industry for the Institute is again acknowledged in the Department of Technology's Report for 1902-03, which refers to the "very valuable assistance from trade organisations, many of which now take a keen interest in technical education, and recognise the advantage of employing technically trained operatives." Bodies still today active in support of the Institute are mentioned, including the National Association of British and Irish Millers, the Paper Makers' Association, and the Master Bakers and Confectioners.

The feeling that the State had now taken over the major burden of financing technical education caused the Corporation of London and a number of Livery Companies to reduce their contributions considerably in 1904: this brought about something of a financial crisis for the Institute. The new Chairman of Council, Lord Halsbury, Lord Chancellor and Past Master of the Saddlers' Company, convened a meeting of representatives of the Corporation and Companies on 5 December 1904 at Saddlers' Hall. A resolution regretting the reduction in financial support was passed unanimously, and later communicated formally to the Court of Common Council and the Livery Companies associated with the Institute. Its outcome was largely successful, the majority of contributions being restored to their former levels in 1905, and some of them increased. The City Corporation and Companies appear to have responded favourably to the case made by the Institute's Department of Technology for increased funding to support the 10% increase in candidate entries, and to develop improvements in preliminary technical education and in the qualifications of teachers.

The increase in candidate numbers (which in 1906 for the first time exceeded twenty thousand – a total entry of 20 610 being recorded) was a direct consequence of the stimulus to the provision of technical classes afforded by the Board of Education's Regulations for grant.

In 1905 the Board of Education published a Report including recommendations on the reorganisation of "existing or projected Institutions for instruction at South Kensington". This foreshadowed the coalescence of the City and Guilds Central Technical College, the Royal College of Science, and the Royal School of Mines to form a new Imperial College of Science and Technology. Since 1903 the Institute had been seeking to co-ordinate aspects of the work of the three colleges, so as to avoid the costly duplication of laboratory facilities.

The work of the Institute's Department of Technology continued to grow. The Department's Report for Session 1904-05 summarised the ways in which the Institute was able to co-operate with the Education Authorities as being:

(1)   Schemes for Courses of Instruction,
(2)   Registration of Classes,
(3)   Approval of Teachers,
(4)   Examinations,
(5)   Inspection,
(6)   Teachers' Certificates.

The Report for Session 1905-06 commented: "The work of this Department continues year by year to grow in volume and in complexity." In the next Report, the progressive enforcement of the regulations to make attendance at a course a condition of entry to the examination, and to have passed the lower levels of examinations before entering for the higher levels, was emphasised. The importance of grouped courses of study embracing technology, practice, science and mathematics, and drawing, was stressed in conformity with the developing policy of the Board of Education. The Report for 1908 returned to this theme, and commented: "Notwithstanding the efforts of Local Authorities in this direction, it is still found to be the case that large numbers of young persons, who have left school at 13 or 14 years of age, apply at or about the age of 18 for admission to Technological Classes, having forgotten a great part of what they had learned in School. The money spent on their Elementary Education is thus to a great extent wasted . . . " The situation had improved by 1910, when satisfaction was expressed at the increase in numbers of candidates for Preliminary examinations, "showing that the instruction now followed . . . is becoming generally more continuous, and that a larger proportion of students attend a course . . . covering at least three years."

In 1910 also, the Institute petitioned for and was granted a Supplemental Royal Charter, to regulate its position in relation to the new Imperial College of Science and Technology which had itself been incorporated by Royal Charter in 1907. The Supplemental Charter approved the re-naming of the Central Technical College as the City and Guilds College, and constituted a Delegacy of the Institute and Imperial College to be responsible for administering the City and Guilds College. From 1910-11 responsibility for the College lay with the Delegacy rather than with the Institute, which continued as one of the two joint participants. During 1910-11 the Institute's Technology Committee was considering the effects on City and Guilds examinations, and particularly on the future of the FTC, of the notification by the Board of Education in Circular No. 776 that it would cease to hold examinations in Stage I of all Science subjects; would give up practical examinations; and would only hold Science examinations in a limited list of subjects.

This action by the Board followed upon its initiation, in Ch. 6 of its Regulations for 1907-08, of a scheme whereby the Board of Education would endorse locally-awarded Grouped Course Certificates. The scheme continued in force under Ch.5 of subsequent years' Regulations until 1918-19, when the Board combined with various professional bodies in the formation of schemes for the award of National Certificates – the start of the provision of Ordinary and Higher National Certificates and Diplomas which existed alongside City and Guilds Certificates from 1921-22 and evolved from 1973-74 into the qualifications of the Technician and Business Education Councils (themselves merged in 1983 into the Business and Technician – subsequently Technology – Education Council). With these measures the end of the second phase of the Institute's history – that of unimpeded growth – looms near. The hint of pessimism is perhaps more apparent to the present-day commentator, who has seen and heard so often subsequently the thoughts expressed at the Annual Prize Distribution in 1912 at Guildhall by the then Lord Chancellor, Viscount Haldane, who said that the Institute's achievements were "an illustration of what can be done and what will be done if people care. What you (the Lord Mayor) and I have to try to do is to get people to care – about education in its multitudinous and varied forms. It is vital to the future of the country. It has the profoundest bearing on the future and much bearing on the present."

The first recorded decrease in numbers of candidates was attributed to the exclusion of insufficiently prepared students from the examinations, the pass rate having improved by 4%. The next year's decline was attributed to "the recent feeling of unrest among certain classes of postal employees" – being particularly marked in Telegraphy and Telephony. From a peak of 24 508 candidates in 1910, the total entry fluctuated at about 22 000 until the outbreak of war.

On 25 March 1915 Sir Philip Magnus retired as Superintendent of Technological Examinations, after 35 years' official connection with the Institute, and was succeeded by Mr Leonard G Killby – who was almost immediately involved in military duties following the outbreak of war. Before that, however, at the suggestion of the President of the Board of Education representatives of the Institute held several meetings with representatives of the Board "to confer as to the future of the Institute's Technological Examinations in relation to the Board's examinations." Memoranda of proposed changes were drawn up by both parties, and exchanged. These "conferences" continued until 1918.

The chief effect of the war, on the Institute, was the severe reduction of income from fees, at all three of its colleges and for examinations. All those eligible, both Honorary Officers, Council and Committee members, staff – and students – volunteered for (or were later conscripted for) service in some branch of the war effort. Technological classes throughout the country were disrupted: candidate numbers decreased by 32% in 1915 and 47% in 1916, to 15 623 and 8508 respectively. The lowest point, of 7405, occurred in 1918.

A further sign of the shift of the "balance of power" in technical education in favour of the Board of Education was the transfer of responsibility for the inspection of Textile classes from the Institute to the Board, at the Board's suggestion. This despite the funding provided by the Clothworkers' Company for the work. The "close relationship between the inspection and examination which it has always been the object of the Institute to secure" would be maintained by the Board's offer to provide relevant information from its inspections to the Institute's Examinations Board.

The Board of Education was also pressing for the inclusion of marks awarded by teachers for class and home work in the results of the Institute's examinations: this matter was under consideration by the Technology Committee during 1917. The conference between the Board of Education and the Institute, begun in 1914, was renewed at the highest level, and effectively overtook discussions at officer level aimed at adjusting certain differences particularly affecting the Union of Lancashire and Cheshire Institutes.

With the future for the Institute's examinations looking ominous, the Institute nevertheless undertook to provide examinations for Prisoners of War interned in Germany.

In August 1917 the Government introduced its Education Bill, proposing the transition from voluntary attendance at evening classes to compulsory attendance in the daytime at continuation schools. The Institute's reaction was that: "A closer relation between school and factory is to be hoped for, that the theoretical study in the one and the practical work in the other may be associated together." (From the Board of Education Regulations of 1905 to the Education Act of 1944 provision of technical education by means of day or evening courses or part-time or full-time vocational courses was regarded as constituting a "school" for purposes of grant. Throughout this period the Board's efforts were directed to improving such provision, and particularly to the extension of the duration of progressive courses of study: the Regulations of 1906 assigned fixed grant to "Technical Institutions providing systematic and prolonged courses of study extending over four or more years.")

The Institute's Department of Technology Report for 1917 was pessimistic in tone: candidates' work was criticised as of poor quality. Attention was called to "the weakness of candidates in spelling, punctuation and the writing of grammatical English, . . . a want of grasp of the question asked, . . . great weakness in calculation, and incapacity to make good sketches." The overall percentage of passes was 60.1%, as against 61.5% in 1916.

The examinations of 1918 took into account, for the first time, marks awarded by teachers for: (1) class work, (2) home work, (3) practical work, (4) note books, and (5) test examinations held during the term. This development included 110 centres and 58 subjects. The Institute's verdict was : "While effecting its purpose of associating teachers more closely with the Institute's examinations, it would appear from . . . the scheme, in which the school marks have been returned on a high and generally similar level, that there is a risk that indifferent candidates may be placed in a position of advantage almost equal to that of the best students."

The Department of Technology Report comments upon the entry of women and girls for such subjects as Motor Car Engineering, Electrical Engineering, Typography, Telegraphy, and Iron and Steel Manufacture, as a result of war conditions.

The chief consequence foreseen by the Institute of the Education Act, 1918 (the "Fisher" Act) was a great increase in the demand for technical teachers to practise in the new Day Continuation Classes. It offered its full cooperation in training and certificating such teachers. In the event the new provision for 14-18 year olds only ever became partially effective, and the situation reverted to the former voluntary basis.

The Council reported: "The future of the Institute's technological examinations, so far as England and Wales are concerned, has been further considered in conference with the Board of Education, and it may be anticipated that many of the examinations in the lower grades will have to be discontinued in England and Wales."

Chapter 3

Government Constraints, 1919-33

The third phase of the Institute's history begins with a major setback. Nationally there was, in the words of the Council's Report for 1919, a "gradual return to peace, but not to pre-war, conditions . . . " In technical education, the greatest difficulty was the shortage of qualified teachers: schools and colleges were brought into direct competition for staff with the industries which they were established to serve. For the Institute as a whole, including City and Guilds College and Finsbury; "The financial position . . . is causing the Council much anxiety."

Where the Finsbury Technical College was concerned the problem was whether or not it should develop along university lines. The Report of the London University Commissioners in 1913 had confirmed that the College was not of university status: in 1919 the Finsbury Professors thought that it was. Demand for entry enabled them to select only those qualified to university standard. The Executive Committee however were unwilling to sacrifice "the eminently practical and industrial character of the teaching to more academic requirements." Alternative provision below the university level was increasingly available in the London Polytechnics and elsewhere – the Northampton Polytechnic was only a mile away. In 1920 the Institute decided to close Finsbury from July 1921, and to admit no new students for 1920-21. This decision was in accordance with the policy of the London County Council Education Committee as authorised by the Education Act, 1918. Finsbury was not eligible for the increased Parliamentary grant; had a relatively fixed income and rising costs; and was badly affected by the decreasing purchasing power of the Pound. On 14 February 1921 the Council accepted a "reprieve" for Finsbury from the LCC, in the shape of a five-year grant of £10 000 per annum. In 1923 the LCC confirmed by letter that the grant would end in July 1926. An attempt by former students and British Drug Houses (BDH) Ltd to carry on the College as a College of Chemical Engineering failed for lack of funds, and so the Council had no alternative but to close the College and dispose of the buildings and equipment. The cash (some £17 000) and assets were distributed by the Council between City and Guilds College, the Art School, and the Department of Technology.

The worst problem arose from the difference of views between the Board of Education and the Institute over the Technological Examinations. The Board, with the resources of the State behind it, could afford to be altruistic; the Institute, as a self-financing organisation run for the benefit of individuals and industry, had to be practical. In 1919 the Council reported the gradual discontinuance of examinations at levels below the Final, on the representation of the Board of Education "that the Institute's lower grade examinations . . . tend, in the view of the Board, to prevent the full development of the Board's scheme for grouped courses of instruction of a more general character for boys and girls after their school training." The Institute published a full *Scheme for the Reorganisation of the Technological Examinations . . . in England and Wales.* The Department of Technology reported that the new Scheme "has called forth protests . . . from several Local Education Authorities and Trade Associations". The Council regretted that it would involve increased expenditure (for a decreased income from entry fees). Apart from the discontinuation of lower level examinations, the new Scheme involved enhanced participation by teachers in the Examinations Board and Advisory Committees; the allocation of responsibility for every subject in the Programme to an Advisory Committee; and the award of examination results only after the consideration of class teachers' marks (as outlined above) and estimates of each candidate's due grade of success. Protests from Trade Associations and manufacturers were "to the effect that a system of graduated examinations of a standard uniform throughout the country is of benefit to industry". Some Principals and teachers regretted the change on educational grounds, "stating that the lower grade examinations of the Institute have always proved a valuable stimulus to students of technical subjects, and have set a useful standard at which they can aim in the annual curriculum of school work." The Grade I examinations in Telegraphy and Telephony were continued at the request of the Post Office; and those in Flour Milling also, on specific representations from the National Association of British and Irish Millers as to the value of the examinations to the industry.

In 1921 the Grade II examinations in three-grade subjects were discontinued in England and Wales, where the number of candidates fell from 9825 in 1920 to 7959. At this time the Department of Technology was increasingly engaged in co-operation with the emerging National Joint Industrial Councils, a number of which acted as the Institute's Advisory Committees for their subjects. In this year the Board of Education inaugurated its scheme for the award, in conjunction with the relevant professional bodies, of Ordinary and Higher National Certificates. In due course the Institute was to be asked, in the Report of the Departmental Committee on Examinations for part-time Students (the "Atholl" Report) published in 1928, to adjust the scope and nomenclature of its examinations in Mechanical and Electrical Engineering to avoid confusion and possible duplication with the National Certificate scheme under which certificates in the same two subjects were issued by the professional Institutions in conjunction with the Board of Education.

From 1921-22 the Board of Education began to allow the Institute once more to hold Grade I and Grade II examinations in various subjects, with the result that total candidate entries again started to increase, until affected adversely by the depressed state of the economy in general. The Council on the recommendation of the Technology Committee asked to meet with the Board of Education to request greater freedom for the Institute to offer Grade I and II examinations. The Board in reply proposed a Conference, which was held on 10 July 1923. As a result discussions involving the Board, the Institute, and Regional and Teachers' organisations continued in a series of five meetings throughout 1924 to consider the centralisation of examining by the Institute in the light of factors such as that candidates (i) were now generally younger and less well-prepared (due not least to the discontinuation of the lower levels of examination), (ii) had more theoretical and less workplace instruction, and (iii) were subject to greater specialisation in industry. The new Labour Prime Minister, Ramsay MacDonald, speaking in Cardiff early in 1924 had said: "The development of technical education is the greatest need of this country."

The economic depression and the uncertain future of the Institute's examinations however meant that the only new subject added to the Programme this year was Radio Communication.

On 20 March 1925 the Conference of Educational Bodies on Technical Examinations for Students Attending Minor Courses in England and Wales published its Report. The Conference had been chaired by Morton Latham, who in 1926 became Chairman of the Institute's Council following the death of Sir Edward Busk (who was also Vice-Chancellor of London University). The Report is a most valuable document for the history of technical education, the development of which it summarises. The Conference had its origin in 1923 (as stated above): its purpose was essentially to clarify relationships between the Board of Education; the Local Education Authorities; the Regional Examining Unions formed by some of the LEAs; the technical teachers; and the City and Guilds of London Institute. It was left to the City and Guilds to represent the voice of industry.

The Report codified the major principles applying to the provision and organisation of technical education up to the Industrial Training Act of 1964 and beyond. It noted the National Certificate and Diploma arrangements, defined "Minor" courses as providing training for an occupation within an industry rather than training for the industry as a whole (a "professional" activity), noted the incomplete and unco-ordinated nature of the work of the Regional Examining Unions, and the two initiatives of 1923 – the Association of Technical Institution's proposals to the Board of Education for a National Scheme of examinations for technical school students and a "clearing house" involving professional organisations, associations of employers and employed, and the various technical institutions; and the City and Guilds' suggestion that its lower grade examinations should be re-established. The Report recognised the influence of examination syllabuses on curricula and teaching, and the necessity to link this aspect of the educational process with other educational functions. It argued in favour of practical and craft work, science and art, in "Minor" technological courses, and that "it is of the greatest importance to preserve in this country the highest possible standard of craftsmanship". The Report laid the foundations of the future system of City and Guilds examinations, by envisaging that:

(a) the Institute should examine at "significant stages", and not at the end of every year,

(b) there might be one, two or three "significant stages" – the norm would be:

Intermediate: the standard to be expected of a student aged 18-19 after two years' systematic technical instruction;

Final: the standard after a further two years,

(c) the Institute should co-operate closely with LEAs in regard to course attendance and eligibility for entry (60% attendances); standards of marking (40% for written, 50% for practical); and satisfactory class and home work: also adherence to the "grouped course" principle,

(d) "education for industry" should involve:

(i) *Industrial and professional organisations,* to define industry's educational needs and state them to educational organisations;

(ii) *Local Education Authorities and the Governing Bodies of Schools,* to provide appropriately and as far as possible for these needs;

(iii) *The Board of Education,* to oversee the expenditure of Parliamentary funds on technical education and to advise and supervise educational organisations,

(e) there would be a full structure of Advisory Committees.

The Report's conclusions summarised the principles of future practice up to the 1980s, of Local Education Authority responsibility for determining whether its technical schools would use examinations administered by the LEA, by the Examining Union of which it was a member, or by the City and Guilds (or other external body); and of the association of teachers with examination systems of all kinds. The Conference agreed, and reported that: "in Minor course subjects the central examining body should be the City and Guilds of London Institute".

The debate continued. In 1926, when for the first time since 1915 the total number of candidates again passed the ten thousand mark (at 11 241), the Council reported: "Fortunately the bulk of the Institute's technical examinations had been held before the general strike was put into force on 4 May 1926, and the remainder were in due course completed, although under conditions of some difficulty and with some delay . . . which correspondingly delayed the completion of the examination results." In this year the Conference of representatives of Local Education Authorities, Teachers and Examining Bodies resolved: "That this Conference . . . , being unanimously of opinion that, while the Conference on Technical Examinations for students attending Minor Courses undoubtedly served a useful purpose, the question of the steps to be taken to survey the whole field of examinations in further education represents a much wider problem, invites the Board of Education to set up a fully representative Committee to explore the whole position of such examinations."

This resolution stemmed from meetings at which the Institute was not represented, the first on 10 November 1925 at Derby, of representatives of Examining Unions of Local Education Authorities at which the formation of a representative authority to co-ordinate and standardise local examinations throughout the country was proposed, and the second on 4 February 1926 between the County Councils Association, the Association of Education Committees, the Association of Municipal Corporations, the Local Examining Unions, and the Board of Education. At the latter meeting both the Report of the Conference on Minor Course Examinations and the resolution of the Derby meeting were considered. The formation of a co-ordinating and standardising authority was endorsed; a Sub-Committee to consider its constitution and functions was recommended; and the Institute was invited to send a representative to serve on the Sub-Committee.

The high level of Government activity in respect of technical education at this time is reflected in the Board of Education's Report for 1924-25, and in the existence of no less than three Government Committees, one enquiring into "the public system of education in England and Wales in relation to the requirements of trade and industry", one (chaired by Lord Emmott) into "the relationship of technical education to other forms of education and to industry and commerce", and one, the Balfour Committee on Industry and Trade, which indirectly touched technical education.

Although the Institute was still chronically short of money, the Council decided in 1927 to donate £10 000 to the building fund for Students' Union and Hostel accommodation at Imperial College, and to offer annual Travelling Studentships – one in Painting and one in Sculpture – of £300 per annum for three years, at the City and Guilds South London Art School.

The outstanding event of 1927 was the appointment by the Board of Education of a Departmental Committee to consider examinations for part-time students in Technical Schools and Colleges. The Board circulated a preliminary Questionnaire, to which the Institute responded in detail, publishing its Answers in July 1927. This document gives a clear picture of the Department of Technology's activities and concerns at this time. The Institute's principal point was to re-state its case to be permitted by the Government once again to hold examinations at Intermediate level in all appropriate subjects in England and Wales. Other contemporary concerns indicated by sub-headings included: "Basis for award (including unsatisfactory experience with teachers' marks); Overlapping of Examining Bodies; Co-operation with Organisations of Industry; Recognition of the Institute's Certificates; External versus Internal Examinations; The preparation of syllabuses; The testing of students' work; Standards of marking." (Lack of space prevents the fuller consideration of the Institute's comments on these topics, essential to the proper conduct of an examining body: they are mentioned here to show the professionalism of the Institute's approach at this time).

The Report of the Departmental Committee on Examinations for Part-time Students, over which the Duchess of Atholl presided (the "Atholl" Report), was published in 1928 and attracted wide interest. Its principal recommendations where the Institute was concerned were:

1 The desirability of closer co-operation with the Regional Examining Unions,

2 The existence of a properly-constituted Advisory Committee of the Institute as a condition of the holding of Intermediate examinations in any subject,

3 The avoidance of any possibility of confusion between City and Guilds and National Certificate schemes.

The Institute's response was swift and positive. It immediately invited representation onto the Examinations Board from all the existing Regional Examining Unions – the Union of Lancashire and Cheshire Institutes, the

Union of Educational Institutions, the East Midland Educational Union, and the Northern Counties Technical Examinations Council – and all accepted. Reciprocal representation was invited in some cases. With regard to Advisory Committees, it was in full agreement. By 1929, when the Institute's official reply to the Board of Education's formal letter of 21 January 1929 about the "Atholl" Report was published on 23 March, the Institute was advised by the following:

(a) *City and Guilds Advisory Committees* for Photo-Engraving; Leather Manufacture; Boot and Shoe Manufacture; Cotton Spinning and Cotton Weaving; Silk and Rayon Courses; Telephony, Telegraphy, and Radio-communication; Railway Carriage Building; Embroidery; Dressmaking, Millinery and Needlework

(b) *Joint Bodies with Industry* – National Association of Master Bakers Education Committee; Institution of Gas Engineers Gas Education Committee; Paper Makers' Association of Great Britain and Ireland Technical Section; Hosiery Training Advisory Committee; Electrical Contractors' Association Advisory Committee on Electrical Installation Work; Plumbing Advisory Committee; Vehicle Building Trade Technical Education Advisory Committee; Joint Industrial Council of the Printing and Allied Trades of the United Kingdom Apprenticeship Committee; International Advisory Committee on Painters' and Decorators' Work; National Joint Industrial Council for the Flour Milling Industry Technical Education Committee; Heating and Domestic Engineers' National Joint Industrial Council Advisory Committee

(c) *Newly-constituted Advisory Committees in consequence of the "Atholl" Report* for Goldsmiths' and Silversmiths' Work; Oils and Fats; Pigments, Paints and Varnishes; Textile Printing; Builders' Quantities; Carpentry and Joinery; Brickwork and Masonry; Cookery.

In deference to the third recommendation, the Electrical Engineering scheme was re-named Electrical Engineering Practice and Mechanical Engineering I and II became respectively Machine Design and Engineering Trades.

The City and Guilds South London Technical Art School celebrated its 50th Anniversary with an Exhibition in the Guildhall Art Gallery of the work of past and present students, from 19 November 1929 when it was opened by the Lord Mayor of London, to 15 December.

The Council of the Institute and the Delegacy of the City and Guilds College both made further grants to the Imperial College building fund in 1929.

In view of the greatly increased expenditure by the Institute on the Art School, the Council through its Art School Committee commissioned a Report on the School, which was presented in 1930. The Report concluded: "We have . . . no hesitation in strongly recommending your Committee to continue its support of this School and . . . to extend such support. . . . We are convinced that in so doing the Committee will, in the future as in the past, confer benefits on a large number of deserving students and enable some of these to achieve results of great national value."

Just as the closing years of the second phase of the Institute's development were clouded by the growing difference of view with the Board of Education, the years leading up to 1933 saw improvements in preparation for further advances in the next phase. In particular the work of the Department of Technology was put on a new footing. Over 80 meetings of Advisory Committees and Sub-Committees were held. Moderating Committees to scrutinise and approve draft question papers were established. The General Regulations were thoroughly revised, to take effect in 1930-31, the main developments being the replacement of the "registration" of classes and approval of teachers by the request from authorised centres of schedules of their classes from which candidates would be entered, and statements of the teachers and their qualifications. The Regulations governing Full Technological Certificates were also amended to admit the examination passes of the Regional Examining Unions in Science subjects as qualifying ancillary subjects for the award.

New subjects introduced in 1930 included Foundry Practice and Science, and Pattern Making, on the invitation of the Institute of British Foundrymen; also Retail Distribution. A new presentation of the Subject Programmes was adopted, the subjects being re-numbered and grouped industrially as follows:-

A   Chemical, Metallurgical and Allied Industries
B   Textile Subjects
C   Electrical Subjects
D   Artistic Crafts
E   Mechanical Engineering and Allied Trades
F   Building Trades
G   Miscellaneous Subjects
H   Women's Subjects and associated Teachers' Certificates
I   Handicraft (Teachers' Certificates).

This was to be the pattern of the next 30 years, although subjects were brought up-to-date and new subjects added.

In 1930-31 the Institute published for the first time full lists of its Advisory Committees for all subjects, showing the Chairmen and Members, and their affiliations, and the Institute staff responsible. The representation in these Advisory Committees of the industry – employers' associations and trade unions; professional bodies; H M Forces; Government departments and H M Inspectors of Schools; associations of education authorities, principals, and teachers; Regional Examining Unions; relevant Livery Companies; and technically-qualified members of the Institute, has been a fundamental source of City and Guilds' subsequent success. No other single factor has exercised comparable influence on the occupational and educational acceptability of City and Guilds qualifications.

The Council's Report for 1931 shows the Institute as a good employer. "The Council have approved a voluntary scheme for providing superannuation grants for clerical (i.e. all non-academic) employees of the Institute. The scheme is non-contributory on the part of the employees and the annual contribution of the Institute has been fixed at 10 per cent of the annual salaries". (This scheme was superseded by other arrangements in due course, leading up to the current City and Guilds of London Institute (1966) Pension Scheme on a contributory basis.)

In 1931 a representative of the newly-constituted Yorkshire Council for Further Education was added to the Examinations Board. Candidate entries increased – as they had done since 1925 and were to continue to do – passing the 15 000 mark in 1931 with a total of 15 586, mainly due to the Post Office subjects. The largest single centre was The Polytechnic, Regent Street, London with 565 candidates. The overall pass rate was 66%, up from 65.4% the previous year.

The main topic of concern to the Council and Department of Technology was the Intermediate examinations. Both "trade" and "teacher" representatives on Advisory Committees were pressing hard for their re-introduction without constraint. The Institute had initiated discussions on the issue with the Regional Examining Unions in 1930, and in 1932 was to report its regret that "no agreed settlement resulted therefrom". On 13 June 1932 the Institute wrote formally to the Board of Education with a general application for the necessary permission for the revival of Intermediate Grade examinations. On 2 May 1933 the Principal Assistant Secretary to the Board of Education,

Cecil Eaton, CB, minuted the Secretary to the Board regarding the dispute between the City and Guilds of London Institute and the ULCI, NCTEC, EMEU and UEI over the re-introduction of Intermediate examinations: "We (i.e. the Board) kept out of the dispute for as long as possible hoping the disputants would settle it themselves. Deadlock was reached in 1932." The background from before 1914 was summarised: the Minute continued: "In the interval, experience had shown Intermediate exams to be educationally desirable in certain subjects. The (Regional) Unions contested the re-introduction of City and Guilds exams as 'a threat to their own examinations of similar standard'."

The way out of the impasse was found in the recognition by all parties of the autonomy of Local Education Authorities to choose the examinations at levels below the Final of either a Regional Examining Union or the City and Guilds. This principle, "always regarded by the Institute as of fundamental importance" (Department of Technology Report, 1931-32), was embodied in the Board of Education's Administrative Memorandum No. 106 of 3 May 1933, whereby the Institute would only accept entries for Intermediate examinations from LEAs in membership of a Regional Examining Union on the specific request by letter of the Chief Education Officer, and would inform the Union concerned immediately following the closing date for entries. It was also agreed that the Institute would formally apply to the Board of Education to re-introduce – or introduce new – Intermediate level examinations (much of the correspondence in the Board's files at the Public Record Office in the ensuing years is concerned with such formal applications, comments by HMI where appropriate, and equally formal permissions).

Despite the economic depression of the early 1930s, candidate entries continued to increase, growth in Engineering and Building Services offsetting the slump in Textiles. By 1933 a total of 16 299 had been reached.

The Council undertook to help towards the acquisition of additional accommodation for Imperial College by a special grant of £1500 per annum for 15 years, and for the Art School by purchase of the freeholds of Nos. 118 and 120 Kennington Park Road, adjoining the existing premises.

This phase may fittingly be brought to a conclusion with some external and independent comments from *Education* of 14 July 1933, welcoming AM No. 106: the controversy started in 1911 on the issue of the Board of Education's Circular 776 which "pronounced in favour of a policy of internal as against external examinations". Because internal teachers' examinations were "not entirely adequate" the Regional Examining Unions entered the field. Trade bodies and Joint Industry Councils made representations in favour of City and Guilds. No further action to extend Regional Examining Unions to cover all of England and Wales followed the "Atholl" Report of 1928: this strengthened the case for City and Guilds. *Education* concluded that the influence of Professional and Trade Associations was perhaps too great, but might be "the salvation of technical education . . . their added interest may be the solution to that standardisation of examinations of which many have dreamt but few expected to realise".

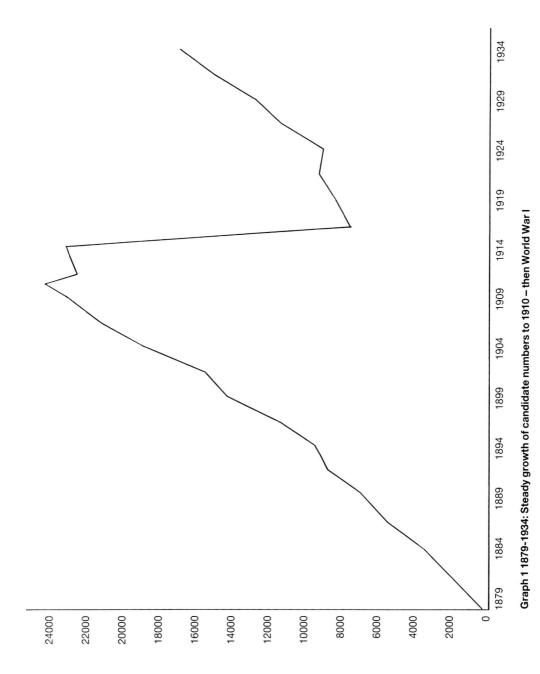

Graph 1 1879-1934: Steady growth of candidate numbers to 1910 – then World War I

Chapter 4

Leadership in Technical Education, 1934-43

For a decade City and Guilds was generally accepted as being the leading authority in technical education. The Institute had achieved constructive working relationships with the Board of Education, Local Education Authorities and Regional Examining Unions, and the teaching profession on the one hand; and was firmly supported by industry and trade associations on the other. With continuing financial support from the Corporation and Livery Companies of the City of London and the restoration of an economically viable pool of candidates the Institute's immediate future was assured.

In 1934 the Institute's Department of Technology reported a record number of candidates – 17 307 in 101 technological subjects from 425 centres in Great Britain and Ireland. The effect of the new Board of Education Scheme is shown in that of the increase of 1008 entries over 1933, 730 were attributable to the reinstatement of Intermediate grade examinations in 11 subjects. Of the 730, 240 were specifically requested by Chief Education Officers of LEAs in membership of Regional Examining Unions.

City and Guilds' syllabuses and examinations in Textile subjects were accepted for the award of Higher National Certificates in Textiles by the Textile Institute in conjunction with the Board of Education, when individually submitted by colleges.

Co-operation with Regional Examining Unions was given practical effect in the introduction in certain subjects of Two-Part certificates denoting success in the Union's Intermediate examination and the Institute's Final. Mutual cross-representation on committees was expanded. Co-operation with technical teachers was expanded, particularly in the Institute's collaboration with the English-Speaking Union and the Association of Teachers in Technical Institutions for the award to technical teachers of Page Scholarships of £50 to enable one teacher annually to study for four weeks in the United States of America. The first award was made in 1934.

Co-operation with industry was expanded, in the introduction of Exploratory Committees of the Institute to investigate and make recommendations on appropriate provision of syllabuses and examinations for new areas of technological study. In 1934 Exploratory Committees were formed for Boilerhouse Practice; Milk and Milk Products; and Dental Mechanics.

The City and Guilds College of Imperial College celebrated its 50th Jubilee with a Conversazione on 4 February 1935, and with the introduction of the award of Honorary Fellowship of the City and Guilds Institute (Hon FCGI), conferred upon three former Deans of the College, all of them Fellows of the Royal Society. (In this year the College officially dropped the description "Engineering" from its title and became the City and Guilds College as in the Institute's Supplemental Royal Charter of 1910).

The recognition accorded to City and Guilds Certificates at this time is indicated by the fact that eight members of staff of the Chemical Research Laboratory, Department of Scientific and Industrial Research, (including the Director of Research, a FRS) held First Class Final Certificates of the Institute, in Iron and Steel Manufacture; Non-ferrous Metallurgy; and Coke and By-products Manufacture. The Institution of Electrical Engineers granted holders of a City and Guilds Final Certificate in Electrical Engineering Practice exemption from its Part II Graduateship Examination. The Institution of Heating and Ventilating Engineers granted holders of a City and Guilds Final Certificate in Heating and Ventilating Engineering Design exemption from its Associate Membership Examination.

The Report on Policy in Technical Education (revised edition, 1934-35) jointly published by the Associations of Technical Institutions (ATI), Principals of Technical Institutions (APTI), Teachers in Technical Institutions (ATTI), and the National Society of Art Masters, commended the work of the Institute and its National Advisory Committees. The Report gave its powerful support to the free access of all students to Intermediate as well as Final City and Guilds examinations. It concluded: "Tribute is due to the City Companies which finance and support the City and Guilds of London Institute in the splendid work it carries out for technical education, and, in particular, for the welfare of the craft student."

An enquiry to the Regional Examining Unions in 1936 regarding the working of the 1933 Scheme for Intermediate Grade Examinations in England and Wales brought the response from the Standing Joint Conference of the Unions, and from the individual representatives of the Unions on the Institute's Examinations Board, that "the Unions were well satisfied."

In 1937 the grand total of candidate entries in all subjects in the United Kingdom and overseas was again a record, at 30 070. The Council stated: "The probability of still further expansion cannot be ruled out of consideration, and it would be disastrous to attempt to check it. This would, of course, involve an additional charge on the funds of the Institute which as the Accounts show are nearly fully allocated; and the time may come, if indeed it has not already arrived, when the Council must take into consideration the question of augmenting its present sources of revenue".

External references to the work of the Institute at this time included the following.

The President of the Association of Teachers in Technical Institutions: "The City and Guilds . . . holds a unique place in the examination scheme on the technological side and with its readiness to examine new schemes with flexibility of mind has done much to encourage the industrial and craft student . . . "

The Report, *Printing and Allied Trades in Scotland*, of the Scottish Committee of the Council for Art and Industry: "The various authorities concerned should consider a common policy in regard to Certificates for students at various stages of their studies. The importance of the Certificates of the City and Guilds . . . is recognised and fuller advantage should be taken of its examinations."

The Principal of Burnley Technical College, in a Paper to the 1938 Annual Conference of the Textile Institute: " . . . the City and Guilds . . . a body which has established itself as the undoubted national authority for craft or vocational education and in this capacity has won the confidence of both the industrial and the educational worlds."

By 1938 the Board of Education had approved the holding of Intermediate examinations in 76 of the 106 main subjects included in the Programme of the Institute's Department of Technology. For 1938-39, the subjects in the Programme were largely re-numbered and some were re-grouped. The Programme for 1939-40 included 140 subjects, the syllabuses of 126 of which had been "reviewed, amended, brought up-to-date and otherwise dealt with by the several Advisory Committees. Of the 126 subjects just mentioned, 34 are new subjects, or new branches of subjects, introduced into the Programme since 1930 . . . "

The outbreak of war in 1939 caused meetings of Advisory and Moderating Committees to be suspended: the latter carried out their work on the examinations for 1940 by correspondence. In this connection a Special Statement was issued early in the year: "Regarding it as a matter of great importance in the national interest that the education of the young artisans and craftsmen should, as far as possible, be maintained at the level reached in recent years, the Institute decided, despite attendant difficulties and drawbacks arising from the war, that the examinations in technological subjects and for Teachers' Certificates should be held in 1940 so far as circumstances permit, and subject to certain modifications in respect of the practical tests and the submission of specimen work. The alterations proposed and modifications referred to were communicated to all concerned by printed circular in November last." The Programme for 1939-40 was carried forward for 1940-41 without reprinting: the only change was in Electrical Installation Work, for which revised syllabuses prepared by the Advisory Committee before the war started were adopted.

The abridged Report issued by the Council for 1940 recorded no serious war damage (from air raids) to any of the Institute's properties. "The recognised standard of the Institute's examinations was invariably maintained . . . " Some special arrangements for assessing practical work were made. Candidate entries fluctuated in response to circumstances. The Reports for 1941 and 1942 describe similar conditions. In 1942 the Department of Technology reported laconically that: "Except at Exeter where the examinations in Telephony and Radio-Communication scheduled for 4, 5, 6 and 7 May, and affecting 27 candidates, could not be held since the Education Offices and contents, including the Institute's question papers, were completely destroyed by enemy action, the Written and Drawing Examinations were held in Great Britain and Ireland on the dates given in the Department's Calendar." This was entirely in keeping with the nation's motto of "Business as Usual."

With the co-operation of the British Red Cross Society and the Order of St John, City and Guilds examinations were held in 1942 at five Prisoner of War Camps in Germany, in 14 subjects and for 75 candidates, of whom 58 were successful. One candidate, Lieut. L M Lindley, gained equal 1st Prize and Silver Medal in the Final level examination in Brewing.

Some Advisory and Moderating Committee meetings were resumed: the Advisory Committees for Typography and Photography met, and the Advisory Committee for Machine Shop Engineering (Machinists', Turners' and Fitters' Work) held a series of meetings to draft revised Regulations and Syllabuses, which were approved by the Examinations Board for session 1943-44.

By 1942, the British people and their Government were confident that the Second World War would eventually be won, and planning for post-war conditions began. The Council's Report for 1942 includes a section boldly headed "Post-War Technical Education". This records Council's approval of the Examinations Board's Resolution that: "The Institute . . . approach the Board of Education with a view to a Conference between the Board and Representatives of the Institute in connection with any reorganisation in the post-war period of the National Schemes of Technical Education for crafts-men and artisans in particular." The President of the Board of Education, The Rt Hon R A Butler, MP "intimated his readiness" to receive a deputation at the Board's offices on 14 July 1942. The Institute's appointed Representatives for this historic meeting were: Professor R S Hutton, Chairman of Council; Sir Henry Steward and Air Vice-Marshal Sir David Munro, Chairman and Vice-Chairman of the Technology Committee and Examinations Board; Mr Walter T Prideaux, Treasurer, also Chairman of the Delegacy of the City and Guilds College; Major W F Pothecary and Mr P M Evans, Joint Hon Secretaries; Mr F F Potter, member of Examinations Board, also Chairman of the Advisory Committee on Handicraft and of the Standing Conference of Regional Examining Unions; Dr Herbert Schofield, member of Examinations Board, also Principal of Loughborough College, Hon Secretary of the Association of Technical Institutions, and Chairman of Examinations Committee, East Midland Educational Union; and Lieut Col W French, Superintendent of the Department of Technology. In the event Mr Evans (Clerk of the Clothworkers' Company) and Dr Schofield were unable to be present due to illness. Before the meeting a summary of points and a memorandum were sent to Mr Butler. City and Guilds' position was summarised thus: "The Institute desire to help in the post-war reorganisation of education for the artisan and craftsman, and to that end would be glad if the Board of Education should see fit to inform them of the Board's proposals in this field and permit them to co-operate in securing the practical realisation of the proposals." The Council's Report continues: "In thanking the deputation for coming to see him, the President said that they were all reaching a fuller appreciation of the value of technical education in its broadest sense and all its possibilities, that developments were coming along, and that whatever scheme of recognised technical education might be adopted, the Board of Education could not hope by themselves to carry it through, but would continue to depend on the City and Guilds of London Institute developing their work on a national basis. The President hoped the Institute would therefore continue to co-operate and to keep in touch with the Board and their officers."

On 20 July 1942 R A Butler wrote to Professor Hutton: "I was glad to have the opportunity of a talk with you and your colleagues last Tuesday. It is gratifying and encouraging to me to know that my Department has the co-operation of the City and Guilds of London Institute in the effort they are making to improve technical training and the qualifications of our teachers . . . "

The immediate outcome of the meeting was the nomination by the Board of Education of the Principal Assistant Secretary of its Technical Branch, Mr H B Wallis (previously Lecturer in Philosophy, Manchester University), to serve on the Institute's Technology Committee in response to the Institute's invitation. The longer-term consequences were to assure the Institute's future place in higher and further education, and to some extent to shape the Education Act of 1944 and the gradual replacement of evenings-only courses by part-time day release.

The Times in September 1942 published a *Trade and Engineering* supplement entitled "Education for Industry: the 'City and Guilds'", in which the history and activities of the Institute were described at some length. City and Guilds syllabuses, it was stated, "guide the instruction given to some hundreds of thousands of students year by year in Great Britain and Ireland as well as in many parts of the Empire." These were named as: Australia, British Guiana and the West Indies, Burma, Canada, Ceylon, East Africa, Egypt, Gibraltar, India, Iraq, Malaya, Malta, Mauritius, New Zealand, Palestine, South Africa and Rhodesia, and West Africa. (Whatever the subsequent changes and advances of these territories, it is gratifying that City and Guilds made a contribution to their technical education and development, and maintains links with the majority of them – and with many other countries not in membership of the Commonwealth as well – to the present day.) *The Times* made a particular point of the close collaboration of trade and industry in the Institute.

In 1943 the Government introduced its Education Bill. The co-operation with the Board of Education initiated in 1942 was carried forward by the submission of a further Statement by the Council to the Board on 1 December 1943 on "Higher Technical Education". This was based on a detailed memorandum prepared by Professor Hutton, and argued powerfully for a more rapid and greatly increased national investment in technical education at all levels but especially at Universities and University-rank Technology Colleges. Presciently, Professor Hutton argued for the reversal of the situation whereby science and technology graduates employed in industry "generally occupy quite subservient positions and the number who become directors or reach positions where they exert real influence on the policy and development of the enterprise are few and far between". The Board of Education was asked to look again at the "infinitesimally small financial provision suggested for technical education" – particularly in the light of "the intimate relationship between industrial reconstruction and . . . education." An equally powerful contribution to the national debate, arguing for equal priority to be given to provision for craftsmen and operatives as for graduate technologists, was made in Notes put forward by Dr J Vargas Eyre, FCGI, an eminent Chemist and member of Council.

To close this phase of the Institute's development some words of Sir Henry Steward, the Chairman of the Technology Committee and Examinations Board, may be appropriate: " . . . the City and Guilds are not only the pioneers of modern times in the field of technical education, but they are the inheritors of the traditions of conduct and the habits of thought by which this . . . country earned its reputation for honest work and gained its position and its credit in the markets of the world."

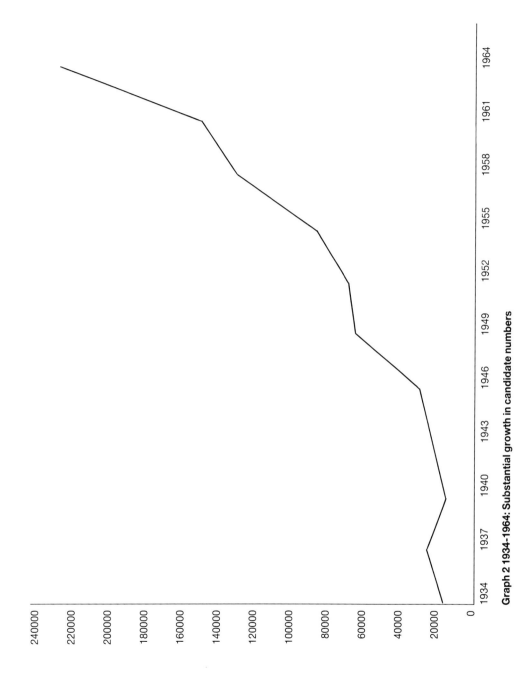

Graph 2 1934-1964: Substantial growth in candidate numbers

Chapter 5

Growing Government Interest, 1944-64

The theme for the next 20 years of City and Guilds' development is set in the Report for 1944: "The Council are happy to report that the relations now established between the Institute and the Ministry of Education are most cordial and very helpful to the work of the Institute."

The statistics of candidate entries for the examinations in technology show considerable growth, from 24 464 in 1944 to 225 186 in 1964. A major development was the inclusion in the Programme of Cookery, not least with a view to the provision of recognised qualifications that would help the resettlement of cooks from H M Forces in civilian employment after the war. The occupational value of Certificates in many subjects was enhanced at this period by their countersignature on behalf of industrial bodies.

The Education Act, 1944 (the "Butler" Act) was welcomed by the Institute, particularly the strengthening, in Part II, of Local Education Authorities' responsibility for the provision of technical education as an obligatory rather than as previously a voluntary activity. The Institute pledged its Department of Technology, within the limits of its resources, to expand and develop its activities so as most effectively to assist LEAs in the schemes for further education which they evolved in consultation with the Ministry of Education (the Board of Education's new title under the Act).

The Institute's strong interest in Higher Technical Education (see above), stemming from its belief in "vertical advancement" from lower grades to the highest for those who would today be described as socially and educationally disadvantaged, and for "late starters" whose potential is unlocked by practical experience of industrial life, continued to be expressed. The Institute was invited by the Ministry of Education to give evidence to the Committee on Higher Technical Education under the chairmanship of Lord Eustace Percy. Professor Hutton, Mr W T Prideaux as Chairman of the Delegacy of City and Guilds College (a Higher Education establishment), and the Superintendent appeared before the Committee, whose consequences were expected "to have a considerable bearing on the future activities of the Institute."

The Times of 15 May 1944 devoted its leading article to "Industrial Efficiency", relating its comments to a special article in the same issue headed "The Making of Craftsmen: Better Social Status for the Skilled Worker: Need for Thorough Training" by George Wansbrough. The leader attributed the inadequacy of provision for technical education to the social discrimination exercised by the country against "the man who works with his hands", and advocated "a radical reversal of that attitude." George Wansbrough's article considered the situation in greater detail, and added: "The present Ordinary National Certificates should be scrapped and the courses leading up to them remodelled. At present – there are honourable exceptions, such as the City and Guilds courses – the courses, like the certificates, are framed (for the most part) as if to give a cheap substitute for a proper technological education."

In June 1944 the Institute's Executive and Technology Committees considered a staff Paper on the future development of the Institute's work, with particular reference to that of the Department of Technology (i.e. the Advisory Committees, Subject Regulations and Syllabuses, Question Papers, Examiners, and Results). The Paper summarised the Institute's early initiatives and history, and the current work of the Department of Technology. It made the important point that in many subjects, e.g. Metallurgy, Dyeing of Textiles, Telecommunications, Electrical Engineering Practice, Illuminating

Engineering, "the schemes and syllabuses can be described as of degree standard in the field covered and requiring quite an advanced knowledge also of appropriate mathematics, chemistry and physics." (Later, City and Guilds courses in these and other subjects at advanced levels in the Polytechnics and Colleges of Advanced Technology were to become, virtually unchanged, degree courses under the Council for National Academic Awards). It stated the urgent need for revision of outstanding syllabuses and for certain new subjects. Specifically, under "Reorganisation of Department", the Paper stated the need for additional premises; additional staff; improvements in publicity, collaboration with colleges (particularly in regard to certification), and examination techniques; and additional finance.

Action on these points was put in hand. The Council's Report for 1945 included a "Summary of the Origin and Activities of the Institute", and graphs showing the growth of its work and (in the Council's words) "the serious falling off in Subscription Income." Finance was the chief concern of the early post-war years. "The additional fees . . . do not cover the extra cost, and in view of the rise in the scale of salaries and other expenses, the nett charge in 1946 against the Institute will be much above the figure for 1945. Unless substantial support is forthcoming the Council anticipate a deficit for . . . 1946 at not less than £4000; and they feel it is incumbent on them to call the attention of the Corporation and the City Livery Companies to the serious financial difficulties that face the Institute." In December 1946 the Chairman of Council wrote to the Masters and Prime Wardens of the 79 Livery Companies then existing, appealing for support. The response was most encouraging, but the year ended with a deficit of £7348 and examination entry fees were increased in consequence.

A Higher Technical Education Special Committee of the Institute was set up in 1946 to liaise with City and Guilds College and with Higher Technical Education generally. This arose from the Report of Lord Eustace Percy's Committee and the resulting Ministry of Education Circular 87 of 20 February

1946 propounding for England and Wales a structure of Regional Advisory Councils for Further Education, Regional Boards for Advanced Technology, and a representative National Council of Technology. The latter was established in 1947 by the Ministry as the National Advisory Council on Education for Industry and Commerce (NACEIC). Of the "Percy" Report the Council stated in its Report for 1946: "In continued fulfilment of the obligations laid upon it by the Royal Charter under which it operates, the Institute is most anxious to take an appropriate part in the further advancement of Technical Education postulated by the Report."

An important feature of 1946 was the presentation of *A Review of the Examination System of the City and Guilds of London Institute* by Mr J L Brereton, Secretary of the University of Cambridge Local Examinations Syndicate and author of *The Case for Examinations*. The Review was commissioned by the Council in 1945, to consider the practise of the Institute's Department of Technology in relation to that for National Certificates and of Regional Examining Unions. The published document gives a full survey and is in the main highly favourable to City and Guilds, particularly commending the work of the Advisory Committees. It argues for increased investment in the study and application of the most up-to-date examination techniques, especially of psychological and statistical methods and the conduct of practical examinations. Comments on the Review were submitted to the Council by the Department of Technology, directed to the practicalities of (a) relationships with Examiners (different for the Institute's industry- and technical college-based Examiners and the academics used by the Cambridge Board); (b) scrutiny of scripts and Examiners' marks by Moderating Committees (prevented by shortage of time before result issue); and (c) the very varied conditions applying to practical work in different occupational subjects. The Review provided impetus for the subsequent maintenance of the highest standards of professionalism in the conduct of City and Guilds' services of educational and industrial skills measurement.

"A gratifying increase in the work of the Institute in all its departments" was reported for 1947. The Corporation and Livery Companies enhanced their subscriptions, which in conjunction with the increased entry fees resulted in a final surplus for the year of £66. The Higher Technical Education Special Committee began to consider the award of a "City and Guilds Diploma in Technology." After much deliberation this was launched in 1949 as the scheme for the Warrant of the City and Guilds Insignia Award in Technology (CGIA), first conferred in 1952 and from October 1990 integrated into the Institute's new and comprehensive structure of progressive awards as the Diploma of Membership of the City and Guilds Institute (MCGI).

The next year, 1948, was "full of useful work . . . the Institute can justly claim still to be fulfilling the need which inspired its foundation . . . ", but once again produced a financial deficit of £1930. The Council put forward the essential argument which subsequent years have seen repeated all too frequently in various forms: "The technical and craft education work of the Institute represents an outstanding opportunity in this modern age for all the ancient guilds to uphold their traditional objectives." A deputation to canvass financial and practical support called upon the Lord Mayor of London.

One significant piece of practical support was contributed to the Institute in the shape of a report on the organisation and work of the Department of Technology by Mr E E Butten, a graduate of City and Guilds College, Fellow of the Institute (FCGI), and Head of the Company, Personnel Administration, which later became the management consultants Urwick Orr. No drastic alterations to the organisation were recommended: the improvements proposed were adopted and progressively implemented, and involved the mechanisation of certain operations and the simplification of systems for numbering, checking and counting entries and handling question papers; the entry forms were modified in consequence.

The appointment was announced as Director of the Department of Technology from 1 November 1949 of Major-General Cyril Lloyd, Director of Army Education for the past five years and a fighting soldier throughout the war.

The effects of growing Government interest in the improvement of education began to be felt in Ministry of Education Circulars requiring intending handicraft teachers to attend approved courses of training, which resulted in the reduction of numbers of candidates for the City and Guilds examinations.

The pattern of increasing activities, growing financial pressures, and lack of public awareness continued. "The independent nature of the control and financing of the Institute are perhaps not widely known nor understood . . . It must be emphasised that the Institute receives no grants from public funds, although it works in the closest co-operation with the Ministry of Education, the Local Education Authorities, and professional and industrial organisations." "It is one of the penalties of our success that the greater the service we give the greater is the cost." Once again, examination entry fees for 1950 and 1951 had to be increased. By 1949 the staff of the Department of Technology had grown to 90, from 39 in 1939. The need for additional premises was acutely appreciated. To promote public knowledge and understanding of City and Guilds, a *Memorandum on the Origin, Development, and Work of the Institute* and *The Work of the City and Guilds of London Institute* were published.

The year 1949-50 saw the start of a partnership that was to achieve a virtual re-foundation of the Institute and thereby to enhance its stature and ability to serve technical education and training nationally and internationally. Sir Frederick Handley Page, the eminent aircraft manufacturer, became Chairman of the Council and Executive Committee, and General Cyril Lloyd became Director and in time Director-General. Handley Page's initiative and verve were complemented by Lloyd's administrative expertise, so that together they created a new perception of the Institute as an instrument of the post-war Welfare State.

From 1950 it is apparent that the Institute has changed into a higher gear. A strengthening of the structure and personnel of the committees advising the Council took place, a new Educational Policy Committee replacing the Special Committee on Higher Technical Education and a Public Relations Committee being formed. At the level of relations with Government, the Report of the Parliamentary and Scientific Committee on *Technical Education and Skilled Manpower* chaired by Viscount Samuel, dated July 1950, was high in its praise for the Institute and its consultation with the Minister of Education, and stated: " . . . there is a tendency for many apprentices and other young workers particularly in the engineering and building industries, to embark on a National Certificate course although they would gain far more benefit from a course leading to the award of the City and Guilds Craft Certificate . . . The Ministry of Education should vigorously encourage the development of courses leading to the award of the City and Guilds of London Institute Certificate in order that the general level of craftsmanship should be improved and that the future foreman should be able to follow advanced practical courses." The Council in its own Report referred to the work of the Institute's Department of Technology in providing for (a) semi-skilled operatives; (b) skilled craftsmen; (c) technicians; and (d) technologists – a classification subsequently generally adopted in, e.g., the Government's White Paper of 1961 *Better Opportunities in Technical Education*. City and Guilds provided or was developing schemes for all four levels. For technicians it advocated "a sound foundation of trade or craft experience reinforced progressively by a study of the related theoretical subjects. This offers an approach, with a practical bias, alternative to that of the schemes of Ordinary National and Higher National Certificates." For technologists, City and Guilds offered comments on the future of higher technological education to NACEIC, and followed up its submission with a deputation to the Minister of Education, Mr George Tomlinson, and his officials to argue for the further development of higher level courses based on a sufficient scientific foundation, and for radical improvements in the finance, staffing, equipment and accommodation of technical colleges. The deputation argued against the establishment of a "Royal College of Technologists" and an associated high-prestige award.

As an independently-minded industrialist, Handley Page was not unduly frightened by an Institute deficit of over £8000 for 1950, and proceeded to give, at his own expense, a dinner for the Lord Mayor of London and the Sheriffs, and the Masters and Clerks of all the Livery Companies, to meet the Institute's Council. The function took place at Grocers' Hall on 10 January 1951 as a public relations and fund-raising initiative.

An event of the utmost importance for the Institute was the acceptance by HRH The Duke of Edinburgh of election as President at a Special General Meeting of the Institute on 21 September 1951 at Skinners' Hall. At the time of writing His Royal Highness continues as President.

With regard to technological education, the Institute's dissatisfaction with the *Statement of Government Policy for the Development of Higher Technological Education in Great Britain* (Cmnd. 8357) of September 1950 was expressed by a further deputation in December 1951 to the new Minister of Education, Miss Florence Horsbrugh. For its own benefit the Institute at this time formed Consultative Committees for the Printing, Electrical, and Building Industries, to provide broader views than were afforded by the subject-specific Advisory Committees. From this time also, the development of technical education and examinations overseas forms a regular and major part of the work, featuring regularly in the Annual Reports.

Throughout 1951 the Institute was represented in discussions regarding the establishment of an additional examining body "with experience in technical and commercial education", for the purpose of examining pupils of secondary modern and secondary technical schools, and technical colleges, for the General Certificate of Education (GCE). A Conference in November 1951 recommended, *inter alia,* the establishment of a "Ninth Body". In 1953 the Institute undertook, "during the initial stages", the administration and financial responsibilities of the provisionally-entitled "Joint Examinations Board for the General Certificate of Education", of which City and Guilds was one of 16 sponsoring bodies. It was planned to offer the first examinations in 1955. The Minister of Education granted the Institute provisional approval under the ruling legislation to examine for the GCE – and recommended a different title be found. On 28 July 1954 at a Press Conference in Vintners' Hall, Sir Frederick Handley Page launched the Associated Examining Board for the General Certificate of Education. On 30 September 1967 the AEB became fully constitutionally and financially independent. While under the overall responsibility of the Institute, the AEB examined a cumulative total of 699 410 candidates, 627 178 at 'O' Level and 72 232 at 'A' Level.

By 1952, candidate entries for City and Guilds examinations were double what they had been in 1946 (69 337 as against 30 889). An important change in the Institute's financial policy was made in 1953. The Council appealed "to those branches of industry which benefit from its work" to add their financial support for the Institute to that given for 75 years by the Corporation and Livery Companies of London. The appeal was launched by Sir Frederick Handley Page on 11 February 1953 at a dinner in The Mansion House in the City of London, at which the Lord Mayor and Sheriffs were present, with many prominent representatives of industry and commerce and the Masters and Clerks of the Livery Companies. The Master of the Mercers' Company gave an assurance that the Livery Companies "would welcome industrial participation in this great enterprise." The generous and continuing response of industry and commerce in the next five years was fittingly acknowledged in the amendment of the Institute's Statutes in 1958 so as to extend Corporate Membership of the Institute to subscribing firms

1

2

3

4   5

6

7

8

Plate II.
EXAMINATION CENTRES OF 1931 IN SCOTLAND

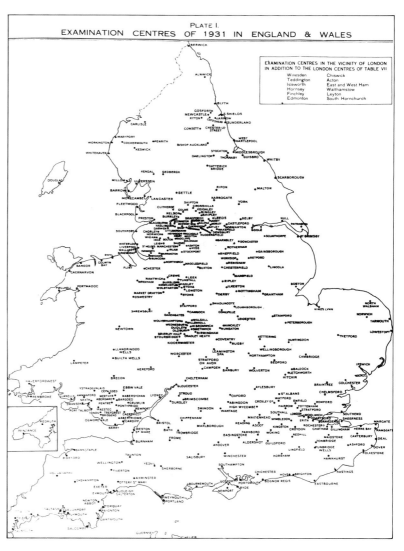

Plate I.
EXAMINATION CENTRES OF 1931 IN ENGLAND & WALES

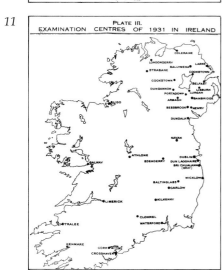

Plate III.
EXAMINATION CENTRES OF 1931 IN IRELAND

12

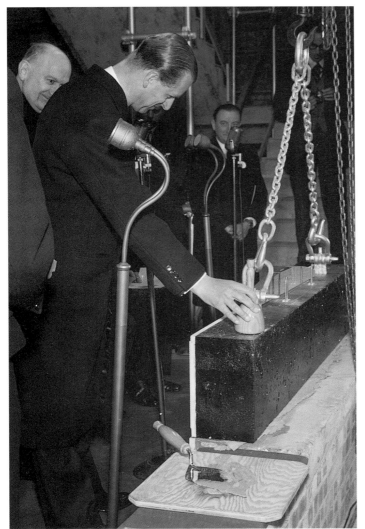

13

14

15

and organisations, and to make their appointed Representatives eligible for election to the Council.

The involvement of industry in the Institute was a dominant theme from the early 1950s. The Department of Technology's Report for 1953 recorded: "The Council are satisfied that the Institute is exploiting fully within its means the opportunity to meet the requirements of industry to which it is increasingly indebted for advisory personnel and financial support. . . . The Council look forward to the advent of direct industrial representation to maintain even more effectively the Institute's tradition of useful service in the technical training field to the Country and Commonwealth."

The Report for 1953 also welcomed the Government's recently-announced plans for the expansion of Imperial College, as part of the development of Higher Education nationally: these plans were to have far-reaching consequences and to result in Imperial College's recognition in 1990-91 as the finest establishment in Europe for higher education in Engineering. This accolade is not least a tribute to the pioneering work and subsequent perseverance of the City and Guilds of London Institute.

In 1953 the Institute's Accounts were changed from the calendar to the educational year ending on 30 September. The campaign to increase funds was maintained. The Members of the Institute and the public were reminded that "examinations are only held once each year and therefore the income arising is seasonal." The pressing need was for new accommodation for the Department of Technology, currently housed in rented premises in South Kensington (see Appendix I). The response to the Appeal to Industry was encouraging.

On the educational front the range and pace of activity were increasing. There was a "marked and unexpected" increase in candidates. The scheme for part-time courses leading to the City and Guilds Technical Teachers' Certificate was introduced for first examinations in 1954. The Consultative Committees were dealing with such topics as relationships between City and Guilds and National Certificate courses; foremanship courses; the position of Liberal Studies; new courses and certificate provision; and the perennial question of the FTC. On the Examinations Board the Institute "has been glad to accede to the request of the several Regional Advisory Councils for further representation", and London and Home Counties, and West Midlands, joined the Yorkshire Council for Further Education in appointing representatives.

Following the change in the Institute's accounting year, in 1953-54 the annual Report followed suit – a practice that has continued to date. The Council adumbrated its educational philosophy as follows: " . . . facilities for technical and industrial training are expanding, and . . . employees are alive to the needs of the day . . . Apart from the interests of industry itself, the Institute's gospel to the young is that the possession of a practical qualification is an investment, if not a life assurance, which should not be neglected in prosperous times."

Administratively, " . . . progress and expansion . . . mean additional strain on a dispersed and ill-housed staff." The Council was giving much thought to "the question of a central Institute building", and to the strong arguments for "headquarters in London, if not in the City . . . " – these being principally convenience of meetings, prestige, and tradition.

Industry continued to respond generously to the Appeal, and the commitment of firms and enterprises of all sizes to subscribe on a continuing basis augured well for the future.

Candidate entries for City and Guilds examinations passed the 100 000 mark in 1955; the year in which the Institute as a corporate body received a grant of Arms from the Kings of Arms by warrant of the Earl Marshal on behalf of the Sovereign.

1954-55 also saw an administrative re-organisation of the Institute, aimed at promoting greater efficiency and co-operation and affording a more positive policy for relations with Imperial College, and greater freedom for the Art School. The Committee for Work Overseas was established as a senior committee to advise the Executive Committee on policy in regard to the special requirements of the growing market for City and Guilds' services outside the United Kingdom. From this initiative stemmed the schemes for City and Guilds Ordinary and Higher Technician Certificates and Diplomas to provide candidates overseas with comparable (but suitably modified) qualifications to the Ordinary and Higher National Certificates and Diplomas endorsed by the Ministry of Education (or Scottish Education Department) and available only within the United Kingdom.

The growing Government interest in the development of technical education and the work of City and Guilds at this time is illustrated by the convening at the Ministry of Education on 9 January 1954 of a meeting of representatives of the Ministry, the four Regional Examining Unions, and the Institute, at which it was agreed to establish a small Standing Committee of Technical Examining Bodies for the exchange of views on plans for new and revised schemes, and the working of the "Concordat" (the Board of Education's "Scheme" of 1933). The Standing Committee would have no executive powers.The administrative changes adopted by the Institute in 1954-55 were reflected in a changed format and presentation of the Council's Annual Report, which in a general review of the Institute's past activities and policy included the following prescient words: "The founders were men of vision and action, who realised that industry needed technically trained men in all spheres from the craftsman to the university graduate and that art could make a great contribution to industrial prosperity. Today, whilst there is a better appreciation of design, with automation in sight there may be a temptation to overlook the needs of sub-professional grades and to think only in terms of the scientist and technologist." The ensuing years indicate how fully the Institute has given effect to its own precept. That it has been able to do so is due to the further response by industry to the Institute's Appeal for Funds. Sir Frederick Handley Page's personal appeal in 1952 was followed by the launching of "a permanent partnership of old and new interests" in the Institute in 1955. Once again Sir Frederick gave a dinner in The Mansion House, on 2 March 1955, at which the Lord Mayor and Sheriffs, and representatives of the Livery Companies, industry, and Government were present. The principal guest, who proposed the toast to the Institute, was the Minister of Education, Sir David Eccles, who referred to the voracious appetite for trained men and women of the new scientific revolution. The Minister said: "We shall go nowhere near satisfying that appetite if we rely solely on public funds and government organised education. Responsible private enterprise has a great part to play, and I can think of no better example than the City and Guilds Institute with its famous college and remarkable system of examinations. All this is due to the far-seeing generosity of the City Companies and of industry. . . . It would be highly dangerous to neglect the crafts . . . it is surely wrong to believe that the modern world can be run by a handful of honours degree men served by a bewildered mass of unskilled labourers. The City and Guilds recognise this fallacy, and . . . are doing an absolutely vital work . . . ".

In February 1956 the Government published a White Paper on Technical Education, launching a five-year development programme with the main objectives of:

(a) encouraging the training of technicians and craftsmen in part-time day-release courses by providing more local technical colleges, and

(b) increasing the number of technologists trained in technical colleges by strengthening regional colleges and developing some as Colleges of Advanced Technology.

(As mentioned earlier, these developments had considerable consequences for City and Guilds, not least in the establishment this year of the National Council for Technological Awards – which before long became the Council for National Academic Awards).

The same month, February 1956, saw the publication of the first issue of the Institute's *Broadsheet*, a termly newsletter to educational and industrial interests and to all concerned with City and Guilds activities which has continued to appear regularly to the present day.

The Institute's continuing Appeal for Funds was sustained into 1956 with the holding of a further dinner for some 200 guests – leading representatives of industry and commerce – at Grocers' Hall on 7 May. The Council took the opportunity to re-state the Institute's consistent policy (which still applies) that "the fee income derived from examination candidates should cover the relevant cost of these examinations but not the cost of development work."

With the Institute's finances approaching a more assured basis from the subscriptions of industry and the interest and support of Government, it was possible for the Council to proceed with its plans for a headquarters building in which to consolidate all Institute staff not concerned with the City and Guilds College and the City and Guilds of London Art School. A long lease of premises at Nos. 76-78 Portland Place, London, W1 was secured from the Howard de Walden Estate, and building operations commenced in the summer of 1956. The building, of steel-frame and concrete infilling construction, was in the forefront of the technology of the time. The accommodation was designed to provide both for Council and Committee meetings and for the administration of educational development work and of examinations. The President of the Institute, HRH The Duke of Edinburgh, laid the Foundation Stone on 18 February 1958 and by the end of the year the staff from the various "outstations" in the City of London and South Kensington had been consolidated under one roof. Such was the continuing growth of City and Guilds' work, however, that almost immediately the new headquarters proved too small and the search for additional accommodation was resumed.

The Council's Report for 1956-57 contained in its Foreword a truth which, although often stated both before and subsequently, is worthy of repetition here. The Council pointed out that national prosperity is dependent upon a trained workforce which, "man for man, is more efficient than those of our competitors. . . . The Institute believes that such efficiency can only be achieved if there is the closest working relationship between education and industry."

On 24 May 1957 the Lord Mayor of London presided at a Reception in the Guildhall held to honour individuals and representatives of organisations whose services are vital to the Institute's work. The principal speaker was the Chairman of AEI – Associated Electrical Industries – Viscount Chandos, who said that despite the Welfare State there was still both need and scope for a vast amount of voluntary work, including that of the Institute. He cited the example of the USA to show that technological, as distinct from scientific, education needed all the help it could get – as recognised by the Institute's founders. The Institute's purposes were described by its Joint Honorary Secretary, Mr David Woodbine Parish, Chairman and Managing Director of Holliday and Greenwood Ltd, Builders, a past President of the London Master Builders Association and future President of the National Federation of Building Trades Employers and Chairman of the Institute's Council and Executive Committee.

The Report for 1956-57 also contained important truths about the Institute's finances: "The outstanding need is for an assured income large enough to permit the Institute to expand its work in a period of increasing demands for technological education. . . . once the Institute has responded to a request by Industry for the establishment of a scheme of training, that scheme becomes a continuing financial commitment. Few new schemes can support themselves within five years of their inception, and many which are of great technical importance can never become self-supporting although their continuance is essential for a limited number of important candidates." City and Guilds has been able to even-out the costs of such schemes against schemes with large candidate entries producing a surplus of income over costs, and thus to provide an important public service.

From this time onwards City and Guilds began to take an increasingly active role in exhibitions and trade competitions: in 1956-57 it had stands at the Fuel Efficiency Exhibition at Olympia, London; the Electrical Engineers' Exhibition at Earls Court; the Royal (Agricultural) Show at Norwich; and the Farnborough Air Display. In November 1957 the Institute assisted with the Building Crafts Competitions at the Building Exhibition at Olympia. Such activities have continued to the present, to make direct contacts with industrial users of City and Guilds services.

The essential educational and examining work of the Institute comprising these services was developed at this period in important respects. One of the principal effects of the great expansion in numbers of young entrants to employment receiving day-release was to make necessary a re-appraisal of the suitability of the existing schemes for the emerging categories of operatives, craftsmen, technicians, and technologists, particularly in Engineering and Building where the numbers were greatest. The established City and Guilds schemes were designed for students voluntarily attending evening classes in order to improve their knowledge and skill and hence their opportunities of promotion and career advancement. Such students were necessarily a minority. The day-release students increasingly coming forward needed a different type of course, that would prepare them for the practical craftsmanship in which their careers would be likely to be spent, or for technician occupations. The Report for 1956-57 continues: "The well-established scheme of courses and examinations in Machine-Shop Engineering which now attracts some 11,000 per annum is meeting a particular industrial need in the training of future technicians. Strong representations were made from the industry that there should be no attempt to debase the standard of this scheme which has a very important place in technical education. The Institute has, therefore, prepared a Craft Course on an entirely new basis, . . . including a high proportion of practical work." This was the seminal scheme in Mechanical Engineering Craft Practice, which set the pattern for the Institute's educational policy and developments through the 1960s. " . . . the new scheme does not represent in any way a 'soft option', nor is it an attempt to do in the technical colleges that practical training, involving merely manual skill, which is better done in industry. The new course represents an attempt to teach the essential principles of machine-shop work based on a progressive series of practical exercises, with which the lecture and demonstration work is closely co-ordinated". (Sentiments of which Sir Philip Magnus would heartily have approved.) A further important principle of general application introduced by City and Guilds at this time was the inclusion of Social (or Liberal) Studies in its published curricula, together with the Technology and associated Science. The aim was to give students an understanding of the place of industry in the modern world, and their own place within it. "The Institute was greatly encouraged by the subsequent publication of the Ministry of Education's Circular 323, *Liberal Studies in Technical Colleges* . . . "

As a preamble to later developments following the Industrial Training Act, 1964 some further extracts from the 1956-57 Report are relevant. "British technical education has been built up on a basis of providing the underlying body of knowledge of *why* the job is done in certain ways, leaving to industry itself the main responsibility for showing *how*. . . . repetitive practical work which serves only to increase manual dexterity and not to widen knowledge has no place in technical *education* but is properly at home in industrial training".

"The Institute's examinations are so closely related to the courses that assessment of practical work is a necessity wherever the subject comprises some aspects which do not lend themselves to written examination and it is possible to organise some form of practical test. . . . whatever the method adopted, the Institute is involved in some of its most demanding and costly work". The detailed review of Practical Examinations undertaken at this time elicited the comment that "the enthusiasm which these local examiners (of individual candidates' practical work at centres) show is one of the most satisfying features of the Institute's partnership with industry and the colleges", but called for the greatest care on the part of the Institute that local examiners were technically qualified and personally suitable, and that standards of assessment were co-ordinated for consistency. The Institute began to hold regular Conferences of local examiners and to seek to perfect its instructions to them. The anticipated further growth in candidate numbers due to the post-war "boom" in the birthrate led the Institute to review its examination procedures. In this it was fortunate to have the assistance and advice of the Director of Studies of the Work Study School at the Cranfield College of Aeronautics, Mr Seymour Hills, and his staff. Improvements in the administration of entry procedures and despatch of question papers to centres resulted. Finally in this process of improving the Institute's procedures, the facilities for in-house printing and reprography were up-graded.

On moving into its new Headquarters and with much new educational and examining policy and practice, the Institute was ready for the formal recognition of its new constitutional relationship with industry embodied in the new Statutes made by the Council under authority of the Royal Charter, and "allowed" by H M Privy Council with effect from 22 May 1958. The newly-constituted Council met for the first time at 76 Portland Place on 15 December 1958, the Lord Mayor of London being present as a Councillor *ex officio*.

On 18 December 1958 the Under-Secretary for Further Education at the Ministry of Education, Mr (later Sir) Anthony Part, and H M Chief Inspector of Schools for Further Education, Mr (later Sir) Cyril English (subsequently to become Director-General), visited the Institute and both addressed the assembled staff. Both spoke most encouragingly about the co-operative relationship existing between the Ministry and the Institute.

A detailed statement of the Institute's philosophy and operations, under the title *Some Notes on the Educational Activities of the Institute,* Memorandum No. 3 was published in October 1958. The Institute's publishing activities underwent a major change in the replacement of Sectional Programmes of Subject Regulations and Syllabuses by individual Subject Pamphlets from 1958-59.

On 13 May 1959 The Duke of Edinburgh as President of the Institute held a meeting of Commonwealth High Commissioners, Government Ministers, and representatives of industrial, commercial, and educational organisations and local government authorities to discuss his proposals to hold Technical Training Weeks throughout the Commonwealth during 1961. The objective was to enhance the attention given publicly to technical and vocational education and training by improving public knowledge and awareness. City and Guilds undertook responsibility for the central administration of the venture, which involved the creation of a network of Executive Committees in the 36 participating countries, operating through governmental authorities at national and local levels and themselves co-ordinated by the overall steering committee in London. A separate United Kingdom Committee was also formed.

City and Guilds submitted written evidence as to its policies and activities to the Government-sponsored Central Advisory Council for Education

(England), under the chairmanship of Sir Geoffrey Crowther, which was considering the full range of factors bearing upon the education and training of the 15-18 age group. Because of its importance as a comprehensive statement of City and Guilds' position and activities, the evidence was published in the journal *The Vocational Aspect* in Spring 1959. One aspect of this interaction with Government concerned specifically the issue of examinations for Secondary Schools, under consideration by a sub-committee of the Secondary School Examinations Council. The Institute's policy at this time was that City and Guilds Technological Examinations, being designed in conjunction with employment in industry, were inappropriate in most cases for use, unmodified, in schools (an exception was Basic Cookery). The Institute was already supporting the AEB, and had a major concern with the standards of attainment of school-leavers embarking upon City and Guilds courses in further education. It was not however concerned to participate in the new Certificate of Secondary Education which resulted from the Council's Report (the "Beloe" Report). In the future, City and Guilds' concern with educational provision in Secondary Schools and with the transition from school to work was to become much more direct.

The Report of the Institute's Council for 1959-60 referred to the significant benefits arising from the concentration of the staff in a single set of premises; and to the development of the principal activities of the years immediately preceding. The single most important event of the year, in full accord with the theme of this phase of the Institute's history, that of "Growing Government Interest", was participation in confidential discussions with the Ministry of Education of proposals arising out of the "Crowther" Report for major modifications to the pattern of part-time courses of technical education. So far as the Institute was concerned, the outcome was rather to augment and to extend its existing provision, than to call for any fundamental alterations. Here the good relations previously built up with other educational organisations, especially the Regional Examining Unions through the Standing Committee of Technical Examining Bodies, and the Associations of Technical Institutions (ATI), Principals of Technical Institutions (APTI) and Teachers in Technical Institutions (ATTI), proved their value.

The main developments to be considered were:

(a) that young people entering technical employment should immediately embark upon related technical education;

(b) that the transition from school to further education should be better co-ordinated, with students being given every encouragement to complete a full five-year secondary course to age 16;

(c) that provision of specially-devised "operative" and "technician" courses should be increased;

(d) that efficient selection of students for "technician" or National Certificate courses should be facilitated by the introduction of diagnostic "general" courses in Engineering, Construction, and Science;

(e) that in consequence the entry conditions for National Certificate courses should more rigorously require four GCE 'O' level passes in appropriate subjects;

(f) that, again in consequence, the preparatory ("S1") year of Ordinary National courses should be abolished;

(g) that the duration of technical courses should be increased, in the case of technicians by means of "sandwich" courses between college and industry; the additional time being used to broaden students' general and technical grounding.

These developments were all progressively given effect; more by action on the part of employers and LEAs than by the Institute. The new General Courses were however devised by City and Guilds jointly with the Regional Bodies, for introduction in 1961-62. Another specific consequence was the replacement of the Machine Shop Engineering scheme (see above) by a newly-devised scheme for Mechanical Engineering Technicians' Certificates.

The demand to drive forward with the new-style Technician courses was emphasised in the Government's White Paper, *Better Opportunities in Technical Education* (Cmnd. 1254) of 1961, and its Scottish counterpart, *Technical Education in Scotland – The Pattern for the Future* (Cmnd. 1245). The first particularly resulted from the Ministry of Education's discussions with the Institute and others. The White Papers recapitulated the developments itemised above, with particular emphasis on the classification of courses as either Operative; Craft; Technician, or Technologist.

The Council's Report characterised 1961 as "a year of exceptional effort" in which the tasks undertaken had "most effectively re-emphasised the national character of the Institute's position in technical education and have demonstrated its ability to fulfil the obligations imposed by its ever-growing importance."

The conclusion of Commonwealth Technical Training Week brought the Institute a message from its President: "My sincerest thanks to you all . . . for making such a resounding success of the . . . Week". In the Commonwealth and Overseas context the Institute continued to play a major part. The "Ashby" Commission on higher education in Nigeria and the "Keir" Committee on higher education in Northern Rhodesia (Zambia) both argued for a substantial expansion of courses for Technicians leading to City and Guilds qualifications. In this field, growing Government interest was manifest in the establishment of the Department of Technical Co-operation to assist the development of technical education in the developing countries. Nearer to home, and of special interest in view of Britain's subsequent membership of the European Community, at the 1961 Conference of the British Association for Commercial and Industrial Education on the pattern of technical education and continental comparisons, Principal H A

Warren of the South-East London Technical College said: "Britain has administrative arrangements which, to meet this challenge of the changing
nature of skill, stand out as far superior to anything in continental Europe".

As part of these administrative arrangements the Institute and the Regional
Examining Unions in 1961 revised the terms of their "Concordat" agreement
of 1933 so as to facilitate co-operation in the implementation of the new
pattern of courses and to improve co-ordination more generally. This
resulted in the formal constitution of the Council of Technical Examining
Bodies to replace both the Standing Conference of Regional Examining
Unions and the Standing Committee of Technical Examining Bodies: the
new Council comprised representatives of City and Guilds; EMEU; NCTEC;
UEI; ULCI; WJEC; and YCFE; the Ministry of Education appointed two
assessors. The first meeting was at County Hall, Chester on 28 September
1962.

The next phase of the Institute's development was foreshadowed in some
words of the Council's Report for 1961-62 that will ring true to anyone who
experienced that phase: "In its work for the advancement of technical education, the challenge of change has become for the Institute an integral factor
in its way of life. . . . ceaseless efforts (are) made to ensure that all this work
shall bear fruit in . . . a regular re-enforcement of industry by thousands of
young men (*sic:* read "people") capable of facing the future with confidence
from the firm base of sound education and training".

With effect from March 1962 a two-year reorganisation of the staff structure
was put in hand. The appointment of Director-General was created and
General Lloyd promoted to it, to be responsible overall and specifically for
external affairs within the United Kingdom and Overseas. A revised post of
Director would control the internal work of five departments: Examinations
(City and Guilds and AEB); Technology (Home); Technology (Overseas);
AEB; and Secretariat and Services (personnel, printing, public relations,
office management and domestic matters).

The close personal interest taken by HRH The Duke of Edinburgh as President of the Institute was re-affirmed by his inauguration on 7 May 1963 of the annual presentation at Buckingham Palace of the Prince Philip Medal. The gold Medal, the personal gift of His Royal Highness, is awarded to an eminent industrial executive or technologist whose career has included City and Guilds qualifications.

Candidate entries for City and Guilds examinations in 1963 passed the 200 000 mark at 200 241: a doubling since 1955. However the Council had to report "difficulty and delay" in re-adjusting working relationships with the Regional Examining Unions, such as to pose threats to the Institute's operations and financial stability. Progress was made in the implementation of the 1961 White Paper, *Better Opportunities in Technical Education.*

New evidence of growing Government interest in the general field of activity covered by City and Guilds was provided by the publication in January 1963 of the White Paper *Industrial training: Government Proposals* (Cmnd. 1892) from the Ministry of Labour. This new departure in an area previously regarded as a job for industry itself was prompted not least by Commonwealth Technical Training Week, which had done much to draw attention to the issues involved and to create a favourable climate of opinion. The initiative can thus be traced back to The Duke of Edinburgh personally, assisted in an administrative capacity by the Institute. City and Guilds responded positively, being pleased "to place its experience at the disposal of the Ministry of Labour". The proposed establishment of Training Boards, industry by industry, was welcomed; as was legislation dramatically to alter the previous leisurely pace of industrial training. The Institute submitted a detailed memorandum prepared by the Educational Policy Committee to Ministers, making the following points:

(a) the Bill should embody an overall philosophy for the development of human resources, and lead rapidly to an efficient and comprehensive system of occupational training;

(b) greater emphasis should be placed on further education which should be recognised as an equal partner with occupational training;

(c) there should be an independent central control body for research, advice, co-ordination and control (of the activities of the industry training boards);

(d) full use should be made of existing agencies (i.e. City and Guilds).

It was pointed out that City and Guilds schemes were ready-made in most instances to be the basis for integrated schemes for recruitment, training, and further education.

As further background to the development of industrial training, City and Guilds published the first two in a series of Monographs on relevant topics – *Technical Education in the USA* by H A Warren, holder of the Page Scholarship for 1962, and *Report on the United Nations Conference on Science and Technology, Human Resources and New Systems of Vocational Training and Apprenticeship* by General Lloyd, who had been Chairman of the session on vocational training at the Conference in Geneva in February 1963. The series was continued in 1964 with *Partnership Incorporated – an account of a joint effort to solve some of the problems of apprenticeship; Further Education for Operatives; Further Education for Craftsmen; Further Education for Technicians;* and *Education for the Printing Industry – a proposed plan for a revised structure of courses.*

The Industrial Training Act was passed on 12 March 1964 – "the first legislation on industrial training since the Statute of Artificers, 1563." City and Guilds' policy was "maximum co-operation and participation". The Director-General accepted the Ministry of Labour's invitation to join the advisory Central Training Council. The Institute's own Council pointed out City and Guilds' long-standing close links with industry, and that while technical education was "a process in its own right" it was only fulfilled when there was also "an equally healthy system of industrial training." The

Educational Policy Committee met four times during 1963-64, and considered topics including liaison with industry training boards and the co-ordination of further education with training programmes; the requirement for new City and Guilds schemes; new patterns of courses and the extension of block-release, sandwich, and full-time integrated courses; the pattern of examinations; and the training and qualification of "shop-floor" instructors.

This phase concludes in a plethora of Government Reports, all of which affected City and Guilds. These, with the Institute's reaction in summary, were:

The "Robbins" Report on *Higher Education*, the recommendations of which, especially in regard to higher technological education, were welcomed as confirmation of the Institute's views over many years and particularly those propounded by Professor Hutton. The recommendation as to Ministerial responsibility for higher education was not approved by the Institute, which communicated its dissent by letter to the Prime Minister, Sir Alec Douglas-Home.

The "Newsom" Report, *Half Our Future*, and the "Brunton" Report, *From School to Further Education*, both of which concerned the improvement of secondary education and were welcomed for their emphasis on the practical and occupational interests predominating with the majority of pupils. The linkage between secondary school and City and Guilds courses was very thoroughly considered by the Institute.

The "Henniker-Heaton" Report on *Day Release* received the Institute's fullest support for its objective of doubling the number of young people receiving day-release from work to further education by 1970 (an additional 250 000). The Institute was somewhat disappointed at the limitations on the Committee's terms of reference: in City and Guilds' opinion the national objective should have been the immediate provision of part-time education for all young people between leaving school and the age of 18, with particular attention to opportunities for girls.

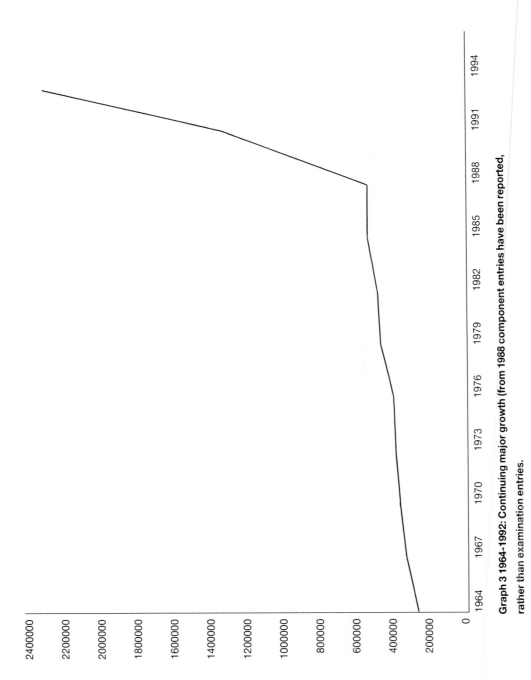

Graph 3 1964-1992: Continuing major growth (from 1988 component entries have been reported, rather than examination entries.

Chapter 6

Alignment with the State System, 1965-92

Enactment of the Industrial Training Act, 1964 in conjunction with the Education Act, 1944 brought City and Guilds' activities entirely within the scope of legislative authority. The effect of this was recognised by the Council, which referred in its Report for 1965-66 to " . . . a new era in which the Institute will no longer itself determine the priorities, but is nevertheless ready and able to play its part." This statement provides the keynote for the present phase of the Institute's development, in which the passing of the initiative wholly to the State, with the consequence that the Institute's activities must be essentially responsive, confronted the Institute with a change in circumstances giving rise to problems of a new order of difficulty. Henceforward, in order to survive and prosper the Institute would have to conform to Government policies and initiatives affecting industry and education in a new order of direct detail, as well as adapting to economic circumstances and public requirements. More than ever before in the Institute's history, this phase is a record of internal developments in response to external events.

Thus while the Institute's Educational Policy Committee was considering the effects of the establishment of the first group of Industry Training Boards, for Engineering, Construction, Iron and Steel, Wool Textiles, and Shipbuilding; the need to relate further education to industrial training; the establishment of the Council for National Academic Awards; and the relationship of the Certificate of Secondary Education to City and Guilds schemes, the Executive Committee was implementing a new structure of senior committees and a related revised staff structure, and had taken the important decision to "computerise" part of the examination cycle.

The introduction of computer processing of examination results data is an excellent example of City and Guilds "practising what it preached". In 1964 an Exploratory Committee on the Training of Junior Computer Personnel – defined as data handling personnel, junior programmers and coders, and those at the next level of responsibility for data preparation and programming – had been formed by the Institute following an approach from the British Computer Society in 1962. The committee initiated City and Guilds' provision of schemes for courses and qualifications for computing and data processing under which the first examinations were offered in 1966 (making this development among the earliest in formal education and training in computing in the United Kingdom). The schemes have subsequently been revised and greatly developed in accordance with the rapid advance of computer technology, and have found their place as an essential component of the national effort to prepare people for working life following the "computer revolution" and the almost universal application of electronic data processing in industry and business.

Computer processing of City and Guilds' examination results data has enabled the Institute to handle the enormously increased volume of candidate entries (from 323 563 in 1967-68 when computer processing was implemented, to 555 513 in 1987-88, after which individual component entries were registered, rising to 2 335 005 in 1991-92), in new schemes of co-ordinated technical education and industrial training arising from Government policies from 1964 onwards to the present; and to provide greatly improved accuracy of measurement and detail of results, all within the established time-scale of examinations. Computer processing has also enabled the Institute to offer examinations at more frequent intervals, so that now they take place in every month, or "on demand", in some subjects. This acceleration of the examining time-table has also been facilitated by the adoption by City and Guilds of new methods of examining, especially multiple-choice tests in which candidates' answers are "read" electronically and the result statistics analysed for consistency (reliability) by computer.

The decision to adopt computer processing of examinations, initially from the point of the receipt from Examiners of their "raw" marks through to the determination of results, their issue to centres, and the compilation of annual statistics and records, was an event of the utmost importance. Work on the system and programming began in October 1965 by a group of senior staff in conjunction with specialist systems analysts and programmers on a consultancy basis from Scientific Control Systems Ltd (SCICON). The new system was completed in time to be used on a "pilot" basis for the examinations of December 1967. The system worked satisfactorily and was fully utilised in May/June 1968. At this stage the consultants' computer installation was used to process data assembled and despatched by the Institute's Examinations Department: in due course a separate Computer Services Department was formed, and the system further developed. An immediate consequence of the introduction of computer processing was a change in the format of City and Guilds Certificates and of the associated results documents. Centres received computer-printed details of individual candidates' performances, by subject, in each question paper or practical (or oral) test, together with the overall result for each candidate and whether or not a certificate would follow. The former classes of result – First Class Pass, Second Class Pass, (or simply Pass), and Fail – were replaced by a new classification into Passed with Distinction, Passed with Credit, Passed, or Failed. Performance in individual papers or tests ("examination components") was published in one of eight grades, grade 1 being the highest and grades 7 and 8 being "Fail" grades. The final decisions as to Pass or Fail, and Distinction or Credit, were (as they had always been) human decisions based on numerical information and experience of the subject concerned, especially of the standards of performance in technical knowledge and skills required by the industry of its candidates.

The computer-based examining system adopted by City and Guilds in 1967-68 provided an essential resource for the Institute, as a basis for subsequent development in accordance with developments in City and Guilds' policies and procedures to be outlined below. Immediate further development of the system to cover entry procedures and documentation had to be held up during 1969-70 pending the outcome of Government's major review of policy and provision for Technician education. The entry stage was successfully included in 1970-71, and in this form the system continued to operate until 1977-78, when work on a new computer system began, intended to become operational in 1980.

In 1971-72 City and Guilds Subject Numbers were comprehensively revised, in consultation with the Department of Education and Science and all other examining bodies, to facilitate computer processing and to conform to a national subject-numbering system linked to a national statistical database. The new system was based on the Standard Industrial Classification. The new Subject Numbers were adopted for the examinations of December 1972 and thereafter.

The first in sequence of the major innovations by the State to affect City and Guilds was the State's intervention in Industrial Training, and the present phase of City and Guilds' history has seen very considerable changes in the means adopted by Government to pursue its aim of improving the quality and quantity of training for employment and in the Institute's response. The second major Governmental departure has affected the whole range of educational provision by local and central Government, and has resulted in a major shift in the scope of City and Guilds' activities away from the upper levels of technical education and into technical and vocational provision for young people aged between 14 and 19. City and Guilds' own constitutional and operational development has taken place in the context of these two major themes.

The Council's Report for 1965-66 stated: "Overall, the impact of the Industrial Training Act on the Institute during the year has been profound, and most particularly in:

(a) creating a need for a formal review of the Institute's range of courses . . . in the light of the respective (Industry Training) Board's policy and programme,

(b) requiring the preparation of new schemes or the radical reconstruction of existing schemes, generally under conditions of urgency, to match new training patterns devised by the Boards,

(c) stimulating an enhanced interest in education and training over the Institute's whole field, and a higher level of activity . . . ,

(d) initiating urgent debate on matters of fundamental significance, concerning the relationships between industrial training and further education.

It is not too much to say that the passing of the Act has opened a new era for the Institute and an era in which the level of activity and the demands on its resources will be greater than ever before . . . " The Educational Policy Committee approved the preparation of a City and Guilds scheme for further education and relevant examinations to complement the Engineering Industry Training Board's recommendations for first year off-the-job training of craft and technician trainees in the engineering industry. This was to result in an entirely new range of provision of Engineering Craft Studies courses, and to have significant effects upon many aspects of the Institute's established and on-going activities, especially upon the development of examining and testing techniques, and upon relations with the Regional Examining Bodies and Advisory Councils.

The discussions that had been taking place with the six Regional Examining Bodies (REBs) on a revised agreement were concluded in December 1966: the resulting document was issued to LEAs and others under cover of the Department of Education and Science's Administrative Memorandum No 2/66. To cement the improved working relationships agreed upon, the Institute formally invited all the REBs to be represented on all of the Institute's

Advisory Committees, and all accepted in principle. The revised agreement was further developed, and linked to the developments following from the promulgation of training programmes by the Industry Training Boards (ITBs) under which substantial changes to technical education schemes were made necessary, in the formation of "Joint Advisory Committees of the City and Guilds of London Institute and Regional Examining Bodies" to undertake the curriculum and syllabus preparation required. The extended agreement was published to the education and industrial training services under the title *Joint Planning of Industrial Training and Associated Further Education* in Administrative Memorandum No 25/67 of the DES and Administrative Memorandum No 19/1967 of the Scottish Education Department. AM No 25/67 stated: "In the view of the Secretary of State (for Education and Science) they (i.e. the planning arrangements) represent a major step forward in establishing procedures that will ensure effective consultation between the industrial training boards and the education service and between the different bodies within the education service".

The effect of these arrangements was to "institutionalise" a division between technical education and industrial training (a matter dealt with in the Livery Companies' Report, *Technical Education*, of 1878 – see *Introduction*), which in retrospect may well have been counter-productive and which to this day causes problems of the funding of courses and the maintenance grants of different categories of students/trainees.

In 1965 a City and Guilds Insignia Award Association was formed on 23 February, "to promote and develop links between holders and between them and the Institute". In July the International Apprentice Competition took place in Glasgow, the administration being provided by City and Guilds.

The important contribution by City and Guilds to technical education and training overseas was fully maintained and enhanced during this phase:

Institute staff were prominent in the Commonwealth Conference on the Education and Training of Technicians at Huddersfield College of Education (Technical), 17-29 October 1966; and at the Fourth Annual Conference on Engineering Education in East Africa, held in Kampala. Co-operation with the West African Examinations Council continued.

In 1966-67 the Council revised the Institute's Instruments of Governance, abolishing the Ordinances made under the Statutes and replacing them by a single Ordinance authorising the Council (or Executive Committee) to make Standing Orders for the conduct and regulation of all aspects of Institute operations. A set of 10 Standing Orders was made and implemented. By it, the Executive Committee was strengthened to assume the responsibilities of the former Finance Committee and Public Relations Committee; a new Committee for Work Overseas was constituted, directly responsible to the Executive Committee; the Educational Policy Committee became the Policy Committee for Education and Training; and the Examinations Board became the Committee for Technical Education (an expression much used by the Institute at this time about itself was "much more than an examining body"). The Council commented that the revised committee structure was "now more representative of industrial and educational interests in keeping with the requirements of the Industrial Training Act". In 1967 Mr (now Sir) David Woodbine Parish succeeded Mr A M Holbein as Chairman of Council, and General Lloyd retired at the end of December to be succeeded by Mr (later Sir) Cyril English, formerly Senior Chief Inspector, Department of Education and Science. The Report foreshadowed a major Governmental initiative, in recording: "The education and training of technicians has become a focal point of increased national interest and the Institute's policy on the education and training of technicians is being kept constantly under review." This referred to the setting up in May 1967 by the Secretary of State for Education and Science (Anthony Crosland), through the National Advisory Council on Education for Industry and Commerce (NACEIC), of the Committee on Technician Courses and Examinations, chaired by

Dr H L Haslegrave (Principal of Loughborough College of Technology, 1953-66). The Committee, to which City and Guilds contributed both written and oral evidence, presented its Report in 1969. The Report and its implementation were to have profound consequences for the Institute.

The Duke of Edinburgh, President of the Institute, presided at the Yearly Meeting held on 19 March 1968. In the course of his address His Royal Highness said: "It is ninety years since the Institute started work . . . Some people may be wondering whether, after all this time, the City and Guilds has anything to offer in this modern age. . . . It is my belief that it has more to offer now than ever before . . . As the Industrial Training Boards get to work, as the technical colleges and polytechnics attract more and more young people who are undergoing some form of apprenticeship or training scheme, so the demand for courses and examinations will grow and the demand for City and Guilds courses and examinations will continue to depend on their realism, on their usefulness and, above all, on their relevance to the future."

To set the President's remarks in their context, the numbers of candidates had grown steadily year by year to reach 323 563 in 1968, and the overall pass rate for City and Guilds examinations had risen steadily for the past 10 years to 71.8%. This was attributed by the Examiners, Committees and Staff to the progressively better matching of curricula and syllabuses to the circumstances and needs of students and industry, and to the increasing effectiveness of college teaching.

The Council at this time put in hand three developments that were to have significant effects in the future. A new senior committee, the Committee for Industrial Training, was established to meet in 1968-69 to advise on the Institute's role in relation to industrial training generally; the co-ordination of City and Guilds work with that of the ITBs; the training aspects of Institute schemes for integrated courses of education and training; and the conduct of tests of practical competence. (The Institute had already as agent for the Shipbuilding ITB devised and administered tests of competence for trainees in metal using and ship joinery, and was working on phased testing of First Year Engineering Craft Apprentices for the Engineering ITB).

Extending from this, in October 1969 the internal organisation was to include a new Examination Techniques Development Unit headed by a Deputy Director, Mrs Olive Foss, an industrial psychologist who had previously worked in industry before joining City and Guilds to develop the schemes for Catering and Agriculture. On behalf of the Institute she had recently visited the USA to study the latest practice in educational and psychomotor skills measurement of the Psychological Corporation, New York; Educational Testing Service (ETS), Princeton, NJ; and the University of Iowa. The Unit (ETDU) was to improve existing and to develop new examining techniques, especially criterion-referenced objective testing; to train Institute staff and Examiners and to offer a service to train teachers in the application of examining techniques; and to plan and introduce a City and Guilds Skills Testing Service to industry and training organisations.

The third project to be authorised was for action by City and Guilds in association with the Council of Technical Examining Bodies to introduce Metric SI units in place of Imperial units in all technical education schemes, over a 10 year period from 1965, in accordance with Government policy.

The Council's Report for 1968-69 returned to the question of finance: "it must be emphasised that the Institute works on close margins." It had "just kept pace with current inflation." The specific grant-in-aid for overseas work from the Ministry of Overseas Development had been increased. The Council authorised an increase in examination entry fees for 1969-70, and once again started a "premises reserve" to provide for the additional accommodation expected to be needed in consequence of the "Haslegrave" Report. Heavy expenditure on research and development in examining techniques in order to maintain City and Guilds' pre-eminent position in this field was planned.

City and Guilds adopted a common policy with the Ministry of Overseas Development to encourage the early devolution of technical examinations to national or regional bodies in the growing number of newly-independent Commonwealth countries.

The principle of devolution was carried further in the next few years: in preparation for the considerable increase in the volume of City and Guilds' work in Technician education which the Institute was given to understand by the Department of Education and Science would follow from implementation of the recommendations of the forthcoming "Haslegrave" Report, the Council decided that the Institute would withdraw from (i) the administration of the International Apprentice Competition after the Competition in Tokyo in November 1970, (ii) the governance and funding of the City and Guilds of London Art School after 31 March 1971, and (iii) participation in the Delegacy of City and Guilds College of Imperial College, meetings of the Delegacy being suspended *sine die* after 1 April 1969 and the Delegacy itself being suspended indefinitely from 16 March 1976.

Publication, approval, and implementation of the "Haslegrave" Report were beset by delays, chief of which was the change of Government following Edward Heath's defeat of Harold Wilson at the General Election on 19 June 1970. In July 1970 the Report was recommended by the National Advisory Council on Education for Industry and Commerce to the new Secretary of State for Education and Science, Margaret Thatcher, for implementation. It proposed a unified organisation for Technician courses, bringing into a single system the existing two "streams" of Ordinary and Higher National Certificates and Diplomas, and the City and Guilds (and in some instances Regional Examining Body) Technician courses — some of which were "end-on" to Craft courses, and some *"ab initio"* following the 1961

White Paper. To oversee the new pattern two new policy bodies, the Technician and Business Education Councils, were proposed. The administration of the Councils and the new pattern of courses and qualifications would be undertaken by the City and Guilds of London Institute. The Institute welcomed the Report in principle, with some detailed reservations, and expressed to the Department of Education and Science its willingness to enter into discussions if invited to do so. By 30 September 1970 a formal invitation to discussions with the Secretary of State was "expected shortly". A year later no invitation had yet been received, and the tone of the Council's Report was "necessarily muted". Proposals for new examination structures and procedures and an associated new classification of results, developed by the Policy Committee for Education and Training in the light of the new examining techniques increasingly being used by City and Guilds — especially multiple-choice testing and in-course assessment — and including discontinuation of the FTC award, were approved by the Executive Committee, but publication was delayed so as not to pre-empt any decisions arising from implementation of the "Haslegrave" Report. Development work on all Technician schemes continued in abeyance.

In February 1972 the long-awaited invitation to negotiate the administration of the "Haslegrave" recommendations was received from the Secretary of State for Education and Science. In April, Institute representatives met with Mrs Thatcher at the House of Commons. In accepting her invitation to City and Guilds to undertake the administration of the new pattern, the Council "sought and received her assurance that the principle of sustaining national standards acceptable to industry would be maintained under any new arrangements adopted by the Technician Education Council and that the Institute's long-term commitments would be contractually safeguarded."

By September 1972, with formal administrative contracts impending, the Council commented on the significant repercussions on the Institute of implementation of "Haslegrave", which "will involve the Institute in the voluntary surrender of its present autonomy for educational policy, curriculum development, and examination standards in the technician field, which cover some 40% of its work."

(City and Guilds' response to the Department of Employment's publication *Training for the Future* issued at this time will be described below when the "training" theme is resumed).

In July 1973 the Institute took a 25 year lease of approximately 41 000 sq.ft. of office and associated "light industrial" (i.e. printing, computer-room and document storage) accommodation at No. 46 Britannia Street, Gray's Inn Road, London, WC1, into which to move the majority of its own staff and services in order to accommodate the Technician and Business Education Councils (TEC and BEC) and their staff in the space vacated at 76 Portland Place. The Institute's staffing structure was re-organised to establish TEC and BEC administrative Departments. TEC was established and its members appointed by the Secretary of State in March 1973; BEC in May 1974. In September 1973 City and Guilds took on from the Department of Education and Science the administration of six Joint Committees for National Certificates and Diplomas: a further eight followed from the professional bodies previously responsible. City and Guilds provided this service until 1986 when the awards concerned were finally discontinued in accordance with Government policy.

Not least of the effects of "Haslegrave" on the Institute were on its finances. TEC and BEC's costs were recoverable by the Institute, but were dependent upon City and Guilds' ability to provide initial funding for current expenditure on TEC and BEC's behalf. In the inflationary circumstances prevailing the Institute needed to maintain the real value of its assets, not just the money value. The Council commented: "The maintenance of the capital employed and the adequacy of the cash flow are vital if the Institute is to retain the ability to operate independently in developing technician education to meet the needs of industry and the nation."

The establishment of TEC and BEC enabled City and Guilds to resume its own educational activities distinct from the autonomous policies of the new Councils. City and Guilds' proposals for its *Examination Structures and Procedures* were published as a Statement of Intent in a Special Edition of the *Broadsheet* in October 1973. The response to the 20 000 copies issued to industry and the education and training services indicated that the proposals were broadly acceptable. They were published, modified where necessary in the light of the responses, as a Policy Statement in December 1974, to become uniformly effective for the examinations in December 1976 and thereafter.

The relative omission of reference to the further education system from the Government's White Paper *Education: A Framework for Expansion* led the Institute, through a sub-committee of the Policy Committee for Education and Training, to prepare a submission to the Secretary of State for Education and Science drawing attention to the importance of improving education and training opportunities for the less-advantaged young people concerned. In May 1974 the Institute submitted to the Rt Hon Reginald Prentice MP, Secretary of State for Education and Science (who visited 76 Portland Place on 8 August for further discussions) a Memorandum on *The Further Education of 16-19 Year Olds by Part-time Day Release,* requesting a full investigation of the situation in the national interest and recommending that the time had now come for Government to implement Part II of the Education Act, 1944 so as to provide a statutory right to day release. The outcome of the Memorandum merged into broader Government initiatives for both training and education affecting, essentially, young people's maintenance entitlements.

At this time also, the system of agreements between City and Guilds and H M Forces under which Service qualifications were recognised for the award of City and Guilds certificates was extended. The work of the Institute's Examination Techniques Development Unit (ETDU) expanded steadily:

the extension of objective testing and the pre-testing of multiple choice test items were the priorities, but consideration was also given to improving marking procedures for traditional written examinations, the determination of results, and teacher participation in assessments. Valuable contacts were established on educational measurement with universities, research organisations, colleges of education, H M Forces and other examination organisations. Institute staff visited the USA and Canada to develop these contacts to the benefit of City and Guilds. In 1973 the Further Education Staff College, Blagdon in conjunction with the Institute organised a conference on "City and Guilds examinations — present developments and future possibilities", in which 35 teachers and industrialists participated with Institute staff. The conference directors included Dr Bill Wallace of the Psychological Corporation, New York, a leading authority on educational measurement. City and Guilds' contribution to research and development in education and the associated measurement, and to the application of the latest and most valid and reliable methods to actual situations was increasingly well-recognised and, served by the computing facilities described above, formed a steadily-expanding part of the Institute's overall activity. The United Kingdom's entry to the European Economic Community in 1973 prompted the Institute to commission a detailed survey of vocational education and training in Belgium, Denmark, France, The Netherlands, and West Germany. The results were summarised in a series of charts of the patterns of courses and qualifications in these countries and in England and Wales for comparison, published by City and Guilds in 1978. The value of this information at the time attracted favourable comment from Government Ministers and Departments. In its comments on TEC's Preliminary Statement and Consultative Document issued in 1973 City and Guilds stressed the paramount importance both nationally and in the EEC context of maintaining consistent standards acceptable to industry.

The Institute recognised, very soon after the formation of TEC and BEC, that neither Council would be content with the role envisaged for them by the

"Haslegrave" Committee: that of autonomous policy-making Councils operating through City and Guilds' administrative and service departments, but that both would seek full independence as soon as possible. Given that City and Guilds had voluntarily undertaken to discontinue some 40% of its examination candidature in favour of alternative provision to be made by TEC and BEC, the question arose for the Institute of finding a suitable replacement for this source of income. (The financial year 1973-74 resulted in a deficit on operations, which was covered from investment income: in the inflationary conditions prevailing this ought to have been reinvested. Additional working capital for TEC, BEC and the Joint Committees was urgently needed.)

As noted above in connection with the "Crowther" and "Beloe" Reports, City and Guilds' policy on Secondary education had for long been kept under continuing review. The raising of the school-leaving age from 15 to 16 in 1972 and the probable effects in reducing temporarily the numbers in further education following City and Guilds courses made it appropriate for the Institute to reconsider the position. There was evidence to suggest that the existing school-leaving qualifications, GCE "O" Level and CSE, were unsuitable for as much as 30% of the 15-16 age group. The Institute started to explore the provision of broadly-vocational Foundation Courses for 16 year olds wishing to continue in full-time education. The Schools Council was kept informed of this development. City and Guilds Foundation Course schemes, described by the Council of the Institute in its Report for 1974-75 as "the most significant new development since the AEB in 1953", began with the participation of a number of schools and colleges in feasibility studies during 1974-75. These developed into pilot studies in the next year. The aim was to provide a vocational focus giving point to the continuation of general education (including particularly literacy and numeracy) and enabling more informed career choice, to ease the transition from school to work, and to enhance personal development. In March 1976 guide schemes in Construction; Engineering; Science Industries; Food Industries; and Community

Care were launched: Office Studies (in conjunction with the Royal Society of Arts); Distribution; and Agricultural Industries were in preparation. The Council reported: "The Institute believes that these courses will provide a major contribution to the Government's efforts on Vocational Preparation". Foundation Courses were fully implemented in 1976-77 with most encouraging results, the majority of students gaining employment on completion of a course. The Confederation of British Industry (CBI) expressed its backing for the courses as a contribution to meeting the concerns expressed in the "Great Debate" on education and industry started by the Prime Minister, James Callaghan, and in the Green Paper *Education in Schools*. Take-up of Foundation Courses grew, stimulated by regional conferences for school staffs, in-service courses for teachers at Huddersfield Polytechnic, and coverage in the Independent Television Authority's educational transmissions in 1978. The combination of external examinations and coursework assessment in Foundation Courses proved highly attractive to schools and colleges: by 1979 they were being followed by over 10 000 students. A survey of candidates successful in June 1979 found that 95% were in employment or full-time further education by November, and that 70% of those in employment were undergoing part-time further education and training. By 1982-83 Foundation Courses were forming part of the new curriculum for 14-18 year olds launched in 14 LEAs under the DES's Technical and Vocational Education Initiative (TVEI), and in 1983-84 they continued to grow in numbers of both centres and students. 1985 saw the candidate entry reach 22 000.

The Institute's independent initiative in developing and providing Foundation Courses afforded a decade of pioneering work in pre-vocational education that was gradually overtaken by Government activity following the radical change of policy brought about by Mrs Thatcher's General Election victory on 4 May 1979. This change included a wider recognition of the importance of better vocational preparation, especially in the non-advanced further education sector, such as City and Guilds had long been advocating.

The new thrust of Government interest was signalled in the DES's consultative paper, *Education and Training of 16-18 Year Olds,* and in that from the Department of Employment, *A Better Start in Working Life,* and led to further proposals for full-time pre-employment vocational courses published by the DES-sponsored Further Education Curriculum Review and Development Unit (FEU) in its paper *A Basis for Choice.* The Institute was gratified that FEU recommended to the Secretary of State for Education and Science that City and Guilds should become the national validating agency for its curricular proposals. These proposals of 1980 were followed in turn by a DES Consultative Document, *Examinations at 17 plus,* which was welcomed by the Institute in regard to its curricular objectives. The Department's ensuing proposals for the management of the new national 17 plus qualification however struck at the heart of City and Guilds' future role and could not be accepted. City and Guilds put forward alternative proposals to DES, which eventually resulted in an invitation from the Secretary of State for Education and Science to the Institute and the Business and Technician Education Council (BTEC) (formed by the merger of TEC and BEC in 1983) jointly to establish the Joint Board for Pre-Vocational Education to administer the new Certificate of Pre-Vocational Education (CPVE). The target date for CPVE courses to start was September 1985. City and Guilds and BTEC both accepted the invitation and the Board was formed in 1983. It led to an agreement between the two bodies to rationalise the pre-vocational schemes currently provided by each, so as "to provide a curriculum for the majority of secondary school students between the ages of 14 and 17 plus which should be more relevant than the existing academically-oriented curriculum that is proving increasingly inappropriate for many students." For City and Guilds this implied the discontinuation of the highly-successful Foundation Courses, which from 1985-86 were assimilated into the new CPVE courses. Foundation Course Certificates were awarded for the last time in 1988, but the term "Foundation" continued in the Foundation Programmes for 14-16 year olds developed by City and Guilds with BTEC from 1985 and implemented in September 1987. The Foundation Courses concept was too important in the occupational "formation" of young people to be allowed to die, and continues at the present time in the new General National Vocational Qualifications (GNVQ) which will be described in due course.

Turning again to developments on the industrial training front, in October 1968 City and Guilds established its Skills Testing Service (STS) for ITBs and employers generally. The STS's initial projects included the provision of practical and job knowledge tests for four of the Construction ITB's new-pattern training courses, and performance tests for Post Office motor vehicle mechanics. The immediate aim of the Service was to develop marketable experience in task analysis and, in conjunction with the Institute's ETDU, in test construction. In 1969-70 this work expanded to provide for a variety of industrial training situations, including the National Craftsman's Certificates for the Motor Industry. Through the Department of Employment and Productivity the STS collaborated with Government Training Centres (GTCs). In 1973, with the formation of a new Institute Research and Development Department, the work of the STS and ETDU was largely combined under a single administration having as its principal activities skills testing and objective testing to meet both industrial and educational requirements.

The Council's Report for 1974-75 refers to the serious consideration being given to the Institute's future role in the evolving circumstances of training and education. Government efforts to combat inflation were imposing financial constraints, through LEAs, on educational funding, such that further education as a non-mandatory sector was facing difficulties. On the other hand there was growing emphasis on the training aspect. In 1972 the Department of Employment had issued *Training for the Future,* stating further education to be "an essential element of effective training which should be planned and implemented on a co-ordinated and complementary basis "(cf *Joint Planning of Industrial Training and Associated Further Education,* 1967 above). City and Guilds collaboration in achieving the objectives of

Training for the Future, including the development of the new Training Opportunities Scheme, was invited. On 17 July 1972 the Rt Hon Maurice Macmillan, Secretary of State for Employment, visited the Institute in this connection. City and Guilds welcomed the Training Opportunities Scheme, "which must not be at the expense of the quality and number of opportunities available to young people". The Institute developed valuable links with the Department of Employment and its officials. By 1975 however it perceived a threat of imbalance between training and education arising from the relative lack of financial constraints, by comparison with LEAs, of the Manpower Services Commission and the Training Services Agency.

The Council pursued the theme of the concordance of education and training in its Report for 1975-76, aiming through City and Guilds' operations to contribute a system of qualifications that would facilitate smooth transitions from school to work, and between jobs. "The problems currently (1976) affecting prospects for employment are unlikely to become any less difficult or to disappear: it is therefore important that improved long-term plans for further education should be developed, and that the need for costly, stop-gap training schemes should as far as possible be obviated". Through the Policy Committee for Education and Training and the newly-appointed Director-General, Harry Knutton, the Council put in hand a full review of the purposes of City and Guilds schemes and certificates with the particular objectives of improving the co-ordination of education and training and the flexibility of course provision by offering more frequent tests and examinations and more rapid responses. The policy review now commissioned produced two important major developments for City and Guilds – a new *Policy on Certificates and Awards,* and a new *Policy and Practice for Schemes* (the latter following a new competence-based approach). The Certificates and Awards policy, implemented in 1978 but not affecting City and Guilds' Senior Awards, was for "a comprehensive framework for progression in a career and for the recognition, at appropriate stages, of attainment in both technical education and industrial training, making use of tests and other means of measuring achievement administered both by the Institute and by other organisations." A consultative document had been circulated in 1976 to which the response was very encouraging.

City and Guilds welcomed the Government's initiatives of Unified Vocational Preparation (UVP) and the Youth Opportunities Scheme (YOPS), and in 1976-77 developed two complementary project-based schemes of vocational preparation. In June 1977 the DES invited the Institute to devise a UVP scheme for the 300 000 young people annually entering employment without receiving further education. This was launched in 1978 as the City and Guilds General Employment Award. The Award was made for successful completion of five assessments involving problem-solving in projects for which there was no time-factor.

Developments by City and Guilds aimed to be of equal benefit in both training and education in hand during the period 1976-79 were the two "free-standing" assessment and certification schemes in Communication Skills and Numeracy, which have subsequently made a valuable contribution to the community both within and beyond the formal education and training structures, to the improvement of adult literacy and numeracy. Measures adopted by the Institute in the late 1970s contributing to a reduction of the divide between education and training also included the conversion of the Skills Testing Service to become "Testing Services", by which an important new scheme for Certificates of Travel Agency Competence (COTAC) was developed in conjunction with ABTA – the Association of British Travel Agents – in 1978-79. While the consultancy and other work of Research and Development, and Testing Services, continued to grow, so too did the more conventional "mainstream" Subject work of City and Guilds schemes and examinations – despite the progressive discontinuation of the Technician schemes.

The changing pattern of City and Guilds candidates between 1975 and 1985 is shown in the following table:-

	1975	**1980**	**1985**
Pre-Vocational	0 (0%)	24 697 (5%)	107 830 (19%)
(Foundation Courses; GVP; Communication Skills; Numeracy etc)			
Technician	166 048 (42%)	113 913 (25%)	0 (0%)
Total	395 483 (100%)	455 836 (100%)	561 841 (100%)

(In 1985 no Technician candidates as such were registered, but a number of Technician-level examinations was held, particularly overseas: the candidates concerned were included in the total under the heading of Specific Vocational Preparation).

In 1978-79 the Institute was engaged in discussions with the Engineering ITB on its review of Engineering Craft training, and also offered comments to the Manpower Services Commission (MSC) on the working of the Employment and Training Act, 1973. In 1981, the MSC's proposals in its *New Training Initiative* were warmly welcomed: the Institute also commented to MSC on the "Open Tech". The next few years saw an increased focus of attention on City and Guilds by both education and training interests. Under the New Training Initiative the training process was devolved more immediately to firms, community groups, and colleges of further education, while a number of Industry Training Boards were closed down as statutory bodies. City and Guilds' services, in association with MSC, were in demand in the preparation of training programmes and the provision of assessment and quality assurance systems: of particular importance was profile reporting and the Youth Opportunities Scheme – from September 1983, the Youth Training Scheme (YTS). This focus on City and Guilds was shown by visits to 76 Portland Place during 1981-82 by the Rt Hon Sir Keith Joseph, Secretary of State for Education and Science; Mr William Shelton, Parliamentary Under

Secretary for Education and Science; Mr Peter Morrison, Parliamentary Under Secretary for Employment; and Mr David Young (now Lord Young), Chairman of the MSC. City and Guilds' Testing Services were called upon increasingly in consequence of the New Training Initiative's insistence on the attainment by trainees of recognised standards of competence: the wide public acceptance of the replacement of "time-serving" by tested skill competence was much welcomed by the Institute. The steady expansion of City and Guilds Testing Services, especially in skills testing, led to the introduction in 1984-85 of arrangements for industrial establishments and colleges of further education to be recognised by the Institute as Accredited Centres for skills testing. (The next major development to affect both training and education, the Government's Review of Vocational Qualifications, established in April 1985, will be described below: it is first desirable to turn back again in time and to pick up the Institute's constitutional and educational affairs).

The Centenary of the Institute's foundation occurred in 1978. In 1975 the Council set up a special sub-committee to prepare suitable celebrations. Jennifer Lang, author of *Pride Without Prejudice, the Story of London's Guilds and Livery Companies*, London 1975, was commissioned to write a historical account, published by the Institute in 1978. The cover of the softback version was adapted from the Institute's Centenary poster designed by the eminent industrial designer Tom Eckersley, OBE and based on the theme adopted for the Centenary – "100 Years' Service to Technical Education." Posters were widely displayed by centres for City and Guilds examinations and skills tests to which they were sent.

The Centenary celebrations began with the Lord Mayor's Show on 12 November 1977 in which the Institute in conjunction with the London Colleges of Fashion, Furniture and Printing; Paddington College; Vauxhall College of Building and Further Education; and Westminster College provided floats showing aspects of technical education and training. The Lord Mayor, Air Commodore and Alderman the Hon Sir Peter Vanneck, was and had been since 1972 the Fishmongers' Company's Appointed Councillor of the Institute. Throughout the year a total of 74 colleges, and 10 major industrial shows, were hosts to Travelling Exhibitions comprising sets of up to 30 display panels depicting the Institute's constitution, history and services. The panels formed the setting for exhibitions and live displays of students' work, usually continuing for several days, during which the colleges concerned were visited by a senior member of City and Guilds staff. To enable the colleges, in England, Wales, Scotland and Northern Ireland, to take part in this programme, 10 sets of panels in all were produced. Formal one-day Regional Conferences were organised during the year by the Institute in co-operation with South Glamorgan Institute of Higher Education, Llandaff, Cardiff; Belfast College of Technology; The College of Further Education, Plymouth; and Newcastle-upon-Tyne College of Arts and Technology: also on 22 November 1978 with Telford College of Further Education, Edinburgh.

The Science Museum, South Kensington, co-operated with the Institute between 2-14 May 1978 in staging live demonstrations of craft skills by some 400 students from City of London Polytechnic (Sir John Cass School of Art); London College of Furniture; Merton Technical College; Paddington College; and Willesden College of Technology. The demonstrations were given in the setting of the City and Guilds Centenary Travelling Exhibition panels.

City and Guilds College at Imperial College of Science and Technology held an Open Day and Reception for the Institute's Centenary on 1 June 1978 (the College celebrated its own Centenary in 1985). The principal events of the Institute's Centenary took place on 31 May 1978 in the presence of the President, HRH The Duke of Edinburgh. A Thanksgiving Service at which Prince Philip gave the Address and the Bishop of London pronounced the Blessing was held in St Paul's Cathedral, followed by a Reception attended by 1250 guests in Guildhall.

The Institute's Founders, the Corporation and Livery Companies of the City of London, were prominent in the Centenary celebrations and generous in their response. The Rt Hon the Lord Mayor was present at the Institute's Yearly Meeting on 9 March 1978 in Plaisterers' Hall, and at the Thanksgiving Service and Reception, at which the Masters, Prime Wardens, Clerks and other representatives of the Livery Companies were also present.

In summary, the Centenary provided the opportunity for City and Guilds to confirm its many links with industry and commerce, education and training, Government both local and national, and above all colleges and schools. Public awareness of City and Guilds' contribution to the development of technical education, especially by the provision of agreed national (and international) standards, was enhanced.

In 1977-78 the Council embarked upon a review of the Institute's Statutes, which had remained unchanged since 1958. The Founder Members in the City of London and the Corporate Members in industry and commerce were widely consulted about a proposed simplification of the Instruments of Governance, to be achieved largely by a reduction in the number of classes of membership of the Institute. It was agreed to discontinue the classes of Corporate Honorary Membership, Individual Ordinary Membership, and Nominated Membership. All the individuals concerned were appointed as Individual Honorary Members – a highly valuable group of people who have made major personal contributions to the work of City and Guilds and who may hold positions of importance in education and training, and a category of Membership that has grown significantly in numbers in recent years. At the express recommendation of the President, The Duke of Edinburgh, the *Ex Officio* Membership was extended to include the President of the Fellowship of Engineering – now the Royal Academy of Engineering. The revised Statutes were approved for adoption by the Council, and were allowed by H M Privy Council on 23 December 1980.

The Institute's Computer Services were expanded significantly in 1978-79 by the installation of a new in-house Data Processing system based on a DEC/PDP 11 minicomputer and an associated optical mark reader, to supplement the bureau services provided at this stage by Centre-File Ltd. The Institute's Computer Services Department's main task was the improvement of the "software" – the sub-systems and programmes for the examining system then in place. Development of a "quick turn-round" system to process "off-peak" assessments and certificate issues was also put in hand.

The new computer system begun in 1977-78 was implemented after three years' continuous development work, in December 1981. It became known by the acronym CIRCE – Computerised Issue of Results and Certificates from Entries (in ancient Greek mythology Circe was a dangerously attractive enchantress). Such was the pace of change in the education and training environment that the Council's report for 1982-83 was already recording a major investment by the Institute in new Data Processing systems, aimed at completion in 1984. All the Institute's computer requirements were to be provided for in-house: the services of external bureaux were phased-out, following the purchase and installation of a DEC/VAX 11/780 mainframe computer, located in the premises acquired in 1974 at 46 Britannia Street, London, WC1. Here and at 76 Portland Place, a network of computer terminals and printers was progressively installed, using the Racal PLANET system. This network was extended in 1989 to the further additional office accommodation acquired by the Institute at 326 City Road, London, EC1. Gradually, all City and Guilds' internal administrative systems – wordprocessing, addressing, information, printing, stock-control and accounting – have been transferred to be computer-based. Improvements have been progressively introduced and at the time of writing continue to be so.

The Institute's DEC/VAX 11/780 computer was first used, very successfully, to process the examinations of May/June 1985. The present Director-General, John Barnes, who took up appointment from 1 April 1985, recognised the need for continuous review and development of City and Guilds' computer services and facilities, both in the form of schemes of education and training in Information Technology for schools, colleges and training centres and in the internal systems, hardware and software and staff. The education and training schemes in Computer Programming, Data Processing and Information Technology have all been radically reviewed and expanded in recent years. Similar processes of review and expansion have been directed to the internal computer services. In 1986-87 the highly-successful vocational scheme in Information Technology, much used by Government-sponsored ITeCs (Information Technology Centres), was augmented by a new scheme for Basic Competence in Information Technology, developed in partnership by City and Guilds, the CBI (Confederation of British Industry), British Aerospace, the DTI (Department of Trade and Industry), and the Information Technology Skills Agency. The Institute's vocational schemes in these as in all aspects of technology have continued to be revised and implemented on a "leap-frogging" basis. In 1988-89 work in-house was directed to the design and proving of CIRCE's eventual successor as the main results processing system, to be known as FORWARD (an acronym whose significance needs no explanation) – Flexible On-line Reporting With Accumulated Results Determination, providing for policy developments occurring in the meantime. In 1990-91 a new and much more powerful mainframe computer, a DEC/VAX 6520, was purchased and installed at 76 Portland Place. At the same time "disaster recovery" provision was made to safeguard the Institute against loss of computer data and records due to accidental causes beyond the Institute's control.

City and Guilds' sustained endeavours to promote national standards of attainment in technical education and to achieve viable working relationships with the Regional Examining Bodies and Regional Advisory Councils for Further Education took a step forward in 1979-80. An Agreement on a Unified System of National Standards and Certification was concluded between the Institute and the Regional organisations, through the Council of Technical Examining Bodies, at a meeting in October 1979 at Ferryside in Dyfed. The "Ferryside" Agreement inaugurated a new era of partnership, implemented in 1980, in which all the Regions would have representation in the Institute's Council, Executive Committee and Policy Committee for Education and Training. The Policy Committee would become "the custodian of national standards." A common form of certificate, headed "City and Guilds of London Institute in association with the Regional Examining Bodies", would be awarded for success in examinations within the Unified System held either by the Institute or by a Regional Body. The examinations concerned were for schemes at Craft and Operative levels.

At the Technician level matters were proceeding less smoothly. As noted earlier, the establishment of the Technician and Business Education Councils as Companies Limited by Guarantee carried within it the seeds of their disengagement to independence from the Institute. BEC had little common interest with City and Guilds and, perhaps for that reason, working relationships since May 1974 had generally been cordial. Because of the difference of interests, the Council of the Institute had no difficulty in acceding, in 1978-79, to BEC's wish to bring its contractual administrative agreement with City and Guilds to a conclusion at the earliest possible opportunity in 1980. BEC's disengagement was effected smoothly from 1 January 1980 and it moved out of 76 Portland Place to alternative accommodation. City and Guilds continued to provide its printing and accounts services until the end of the financial year on 30 September.

BEC's departure could not but be a precedent for that of TEC. Despite the aspirations of the "Haslegrave" Committee – and of the Institute – to achieve a coherent and progressive pattern based on City and Guilds' Technician schemes and examinations rather than the National Certificate and Diploma system, TEC had adopted a pattern involving new levels of qualifications based on the validation of college-devised curricula, syllabuses and examinations within its own new framework. City and Guilds implemented this new system in accordance with its contract, and by 1980 had registered some 151 000 students; issued some 20 000 TEC National awards; and was starting on the third major phase, that of Higher award programmes in all industry sectors. TEC showed little inclination to respond to the Institute's attempts to establish a dialogue on progression and areas of interaction, and in 1980 served notice of its intention to disengage from its administrative agreement with City and Guilds. In 1981 TEC became fully independent of City and Guilds and withdrew to its own premises, taking with it by arrangement upwards of 60 members of staff who had been recruited by the Institute in order to carry out the terms of its contract. TEC indemnified the Institute for the premature termination of the contract. In 1983 BEC and TEC merged to form BTEC.

To return to the heart of City and Guilds' traditional "mainstream" activity, that of publishing schemes for courses of technical education and related examinations, as mentioned above the Policy Committee for Education and Training had initiated a comprehensive review of the purposes of City and Guilds schemes and certificates in 1976. The policy on Certificates and Awards was the first to be completed: the rapid rate at which major external changes were occurring and the need to maintain the availability of City and Guilds examinations prolonged the fundamental review of Institute schemes, in which not only the interface with TEC activities and developments in industrial training but also more basic trends such as the wide adoption of micro-processors, the development of Craft Supplementary Studies, and the focus on specific skills, all prompted by the training agencies (MSC, TSA and ITBs) had to be taken into account. By 1979-80 the Senior Committees were considering the draft policy statement giving guidance on the presentation of schemes of regulations and syllabuses: the next year the draft was widely circulated to the Regional Bodies, colleges, industry and training agencies and much helpful comment on which to base the final version was received.

The "Ferryside" Agreement and contemporaneous developments in the education and training environment led to a decision to review the Institute's structure of Joint Advisory Committees with the Regions and to establish instead National Advisory Committees for each major industry sector or field of activity; and to revise existing schemes in the light of the Policy Statement, the introduction of new technologies and new forms of assessment, and particularly the move towards a process-competence based approach to technical education as an alternative to the traditional subject-based approach. By September 1980 most of the existing Engineering Craft Studies schemes adopted as much as 12 years previously had been re-stated in terms of learning objectives, taking into account changes that had occurred in the meantime and providing for the Institute's new examination structures and procedures. The Joint Advisory Committee for Engineering then formed a Policy Steering Sub-Committee to make recommendations for the future as to the structure and range of schemes for those using craft skills appropriate to the needs of the engineering industry in the 1980s. The Council's Report for 1981-82 recorded its approval of the implementation of a new process-competence based system of technical education, arising from the Sub-Committee's proposals, that would have far-reaching consequences for City and Guilds schemes not only in Engineering but also in Construction, Catering, and eventually in all aspects. The new system was designed to address the problems confronting students as the result of current changes in the economic and employment environment – problems of access to; progression within; and transfer between, both job opportunities and relevant further education courses. Analysis of the existing craft schemes showed much common content of process skills and science underlying the technology as applied by "craftspersons" in different industries. In the new system common content and competencies would be taught and tested together, thus facilitating the provision of viable courses and reducing the duplication of teaching and examining. Crucially, job-relevant certification by City and Guilds would be retained. The progressive conversion of curricula and syllabuses to the new process-competence based approach, in keeping with the new public acceptance of increased emphasis on skill competence, continued throughout 1982-83 for all City and Guilds schemes of specific vocational preparation. At this time the Scottish Education Department was introducing its own separate modular plan for further education in Scotland which was to raise the issue of crossborder certification: City and Guilds courses and examinations would no longer be appropriate in Scotland, and this led to the adoption of measures for closer co-ordination, initially through a new Scottish Consultative Committee formed by the Institute, and later to an Agreement with the Scottish Vocational Education Council (SCOTVEC) on a system of Equivalences whereby Scottish students successful in prescribed modules and wishing to enhance their employment prospects outside Scotland by possession of a City and Guilds qualification could qualify for the endorsement of their SCOTVEC certificates.

These developments in City and Guilds' specific vocational preparation activities were augmented in 1983-84 by the resumption of services at the Technician level. When City and Guilds voluntarily discontinued its Technician schemes in the United Kingdom following the establishment of TEC, it had continued to offer them for overseas centres and candidates: now they were again made available in a modified form in the UK.

The innovations and changes in City and Guilds' computer facilities and education and training provision at the pre-vocational and specific vocational stages so far described took place against the continuing backcloth of Yearly and Council Meetings; a steadily-growing volume of committee activity; and full programmes of work in Research and Development, Testing Services, Consultancy, Publicity and Publications, Conferences and Exhibitions, and services overseas, to H M Forces, and to such special areas as Adult Education and Teachers' Certificates, Creative Studies, and Recreational and Leisure Activities, of which lack of space forbids more than the barest mention. Since the Centenary Year, amounts of subscriptions and donations to the Institute as a registered charity had also once more been steadily growing, confirming the continued support of the City Corporation and Livery Companies, and of industry and commerce, for City and Guilds' growing range of education and training services.

In April 1985 two related events of the greatest importance to the Institute occurred: John Barnes took up appointment as Director-General, and the Government established its Review of Vocational Qualifications by a Working Group of which Mr Barnes was a member. John Barnes had previously been Chief Education Officer of the City of Salford, and before that of Wakefield, and came to City and Guilds with wide experience and a high reputation in both education and industrial training. The aim of the Review of Vocational Qualifications (RVQ) was to improve the national structure of vocational qualifications as the basis for (a) improved recognition of the ability to apply knowledge and skill, and (b) increased opportunities of mobility and progression in employment. The Review was sponsored equally by the Department of Education and Science and the Department of Employment. City and Guilds' activities would clearly be central to its concerns. In an Interim Report the Working Group proposed a collaborative approach by all the organisations involved - City and Guilds, BTEC, the Royal Society of Arts, Regional and other examining bodies such as the Pitman Examinations Institute and the London Chamber of Commerce and Industry, and the industrial training interests – to a new mechanism for the development of a coherent system of assessment and certification.

The Council's Report for 1984-85 described the year as one "of great activity and change, characterised by an outward-looking spirit of co-operation and partnership with other organisations . . . also active in technical and vocational education and training." During the year, Agreements were entered into with BTEC on joint arrangements for Pre-Vocational Education for 14-16 year-olds and on joint Overseas Operations; and with SCOTVEC on the endorsement of City and Guilds Equivalencies on the new Scottish National

Certificates. Discussions were held with ITBs on joint certification of knowledge and competence, and with the Regions on the review of the Unified System of National Standards and Certification. After discussions going back to 1973 on the future of Agricultural Education, progress was made towards the establishment of the National Examinations Board for Agriculture, Horticulture and Allied Industries (NEBAHAI), to be administered by City and Guilds, itself a pioneer in agricultural education from 1949. City and Guilds' involvement in the MSC's new two-year Youth Training Scheme (YTS) was developed through the provision of the General Abilities Profile and, in the next year, the establishment of the YTS Certification Board covering relevant City and Guilds, BTEC, RSA and SCOTVEC qualifications.

The RVQ Report was published in April 1986 and was immediately followed by a joint Department of Employment/Department of Education and Science White Paper, *Working together – Education and Training*. The White Paper was followed directly by the establishment of the National Council for Vocational Qualifications (NCVQ). The Institute's Council in its Report for 1985-86 stated that City and Guilds' major external concern was to contribute to the Review of Vocational Qualifications, and it looked forward to the future integration of City and Guilds qualifications in the new framework of National Vocational Qualifications (NVQ) to be promulgated by the newly-constituted NCVQ. The Institute noted the major transformation occurring in the British economy with reference particularly to Information Technology (IT) and Robotics, and to Travel, Tourism and related services, and committed itself to the continuation, in the new circumstances, of City and Guilds' traditional capability to provide curricula and qualifications to meet the requirements of the economy and the labour market, based on the identified needs of industry and commerce. City and Guilds provided "an important national resource in education", and was therefore a major asset to employment and the economy.

Progress with the system of collaborative agreements continued: NEBAHAI was established on 16 December 1985, and individual agreements were made with the Regional organisations. Partnership agreements expanded to include ITBs and the Institute of Training Development. With future requirements in mind, the Research and Development Department started work on credit transfer and credit accumulation systems.

The first Certificates of Pre-Vocational Education were awarded at a special event held on a riverboat on the River Thames in July 1986 by the Secretary of State for Education and Science, the Rt Hon Kenneth Baker.

1986 had been designated "Industry Year" in a campaign to stress the importance of industry to the British economy sponsored by the Royal Society of Arts: the Institute's contribution was to put on a programme of "Skills in Action" in conjunction with the Science Museum.

The National Council for Vocational Qualifications was established on 1 October 1986 by the Secretaries of State for Employment and for Education and Science, and was charged to rationalise vocational qualifications on a national pattern and to relate them to the agreed needs of industry through "lead bodies" – industrial organisations designated or constituted for the purpose. In July 1987 NCVQ announced its first group of accredited qualifications, all of which included City and Guilds certificates, in Electrical Contracting, Motor Vehicle Maintenance and Repair, Hotel and Catering, and Retail Travel. City and Guilds also undertook research for NCVQ as a basis for its Policy Statements, particularly on Skills Testing, in which City and Guilds' expertise was acknowledged. Close, participative, and constructive relationships between NCVQ and City and Guilds were progressively developed and have been steadily maintained ever since.

1986-87 was a significant year for the Institute, in which the endorsement of its work by industry and education created new challenges and led to changes in established procedures and services. The Institute's financial position was secure. It welcomed the reform of the school education system in hand by the Government, as a contribution to providing a more effective basis for new competencies for working life. City and Guilds was taking a full part in the major external developments initiated by the Government and its agencies, referred to by the Council in its Report as "these important national advances" – principally NVQ; the YTS Certification Board; the Job Training Scheme (JTS) for the long-term unemployed; and CPVE. A new basis of Credit Accumulation was introduced for City and Guilds examinations. Regional Agreements had been concluded with the West Midlands Advisory Council; Yorkshire and Humberside Association for Further and Higher Education; Northern Council for Further Education – also a collaborative Agreement with the Welsh Joint Education Committee.

On 25 November 1986 Mrs Angela Rumbold, Minister of State for Education and Science, visited City and Guilds' offices both at 76 Portland Place and at 46 Britannia Street, and met the Chairman of Council, Honorary Officers, Director-General and staff. Topics of discussion included the Government's proposals for the National Curriculum 5-16, in which the inclusion of Maths, Science and Technology for all pupils was warmly welcomed by the Institute, and the White Paper *Higher Education - Meeting the Challenge,* in response to which City and Guilds hoped that wider access to Higher Education might be made available to industry-based, part-time students holding City and Guilds qualifications.

City and Guilds' contribution to Information Technology was generously acknowledged by the Minister of State for Industry and IT, Mr Geoffrey Pattie, when he opened an exhibition at Portsmouth ITeC and presented the first 35 City and Guilds Certificates of Basic Competence in Information Technology.

On 6 December 1986 the Secretary of State for Employment, Lord Young, was present at the signing of an Agreement on joint certification for Robotics between City and Guilds and ORT (Organisation for Rehabilitation through Training).

Among these constructive developments the only real cause for concern at this time was the constraint imposed on the take-up of CPVE in colleges of further education by competition from BTEC First Awards in Business Studies, and Distribution, for students aged 16 plus. This was the more disappointing because BTEC was the joint sponsoring body with City and Guilds of the Joint Board for Pre-Vocational Education by which CPVE was administered, and the competition was maintained on the basis of a narrowly legalistic interpretation of the distinction between "Pre-Vocational" and "Vocational" Education. The difficulty was to grow, and to lead successively to the withdrawal of BTEC from co-operation with the Institute in the Joint Board and in other joint ventures including overseas operations. This process of disengagement was not completed until 1992. Given the independent aspirations of TEC and BEC from the beginning, disengagement was the inevitable conclusion.

In an "Afterword" to the Report for 1986-87 headed "A Look to the Future" John Barnes stressed City and Guilds' own independence as the Institute's greatest single asset, enabling it to be entirely impartial in its assessments and certification, the public credibility of which was based upon the Institute's unique record of experience and breadth of contacts in education and industry. The keynote for the future was to maintain standards in an operational system affording enhanced flexibility of assessment appropriate to future patterns of study on a unit-base or by open or distance learning, whether industry-based or in further education colleges and schools.

In 1988 the Institute published its strategic forward plan, *City and Guilds: the Next Five Years, 1988-1993,* which attracted much favourable and constructive comment. (Previous corporate plans had been restricted to use as confidential internal working documents). The Secretary of State for Education and Science, the Rt Hon Kenneth Baker, visited the Institute: City and Guilds welcomed his Education Reform Bill in principle, and was co-operating with the National Curriculum Council and the Schools Examinations and Assessment Council. With regard to the proposed Council for Management Education, City and Guilds favoured a national pattern of management education and training built into the NVQ framework.

In "mainstream" vocational education City and Guilds continued to co-operate with the Regional Advisory Councils in the Unified System of National Standards and Certification, the interim arrangements for which through the Council of Technical Examining Bodies came to an end in July 1988, to be replaced by individual formal Agreements with the RACs, eight out of ten of which had been completed by 30 September. The role of colleges of further education was perceived to be changing, relative to the provision of organised training in industry and by Managing Agents accredited by MSC as independent providers. Student numbers overall were declining due to demographic factors. City and Guilds certificates were being accredited in growing numbers for use in both YTS and NVQ. With effect from March 1988 all City and Guilds examinations were based on Credit Accumulation, and the Institute was exploring future arrangements for the Accreditation of Prior Learning (APL). In preparation for the open employment market to be created by the EEC at the end of 1992, the Institute inaugurated a preliminary exploration of the comparability of qualifications. In preparation for the 1989 International Youth Skill Olympics (the former International Apprentice Competition) to be held at the National Exhibition Centre in Birmingham, a contractual agreement for the provision of accommodation and services was entered into with Skill-UK Ltd, the British administering agency.

In Pre-Vocational Education, the Joint Board completed the CPVE Evaluation Report with help from the Department of Education and Science, and modified the scheme in consequence, including provision for two-year courses.

The Council's Report for 1988-89, on the theme of "Quality for a Competitive World" (since 1986-87 the Reports had been based on an identified theme appropriate to the year, the first being "Towards Competence"), recorded the Institute's strong financial position and reaffirmed City and Guilds' commitment to improving standards – at home in collaboration with NCVQ, and internationally in co-operation with local organisations to develop standard-setting and testing systems. With NCVQ, an ever-increasing number of City and Guilds schemes were being accredited as NVQ. The Institute was providing consultancy services in connection with Credit Accumulation, Accreditation of Prior Learning, and a national qualifications database; and was co-operating with the designated Lead Industry Bodies. Consultancy services overseas were progressively replacing the provision of examinations specially devised for overseas circumstances. Altogether, the Institute was able to report an increased range of collaborative Agreements with organisations in industry, commerce and the public services: specifically, the range of Regional Agreements to carry forward the Unified System of National Standards and Certification had been completed. New schemes in Business Administration and for Retail Certificates (jointly with the National Retail Training Council) had been introduced. A most important advance following the Education Reform Act, 1988 was the approval by the Schools Examinations and Assessment Council (SEAC) of City and Guilds schemes in English, Maths and Science as equivalents to the General Certificate of Secondary Education (GCSE) which replaced the former GCE "O" level and Certificate of Secondary Education. The City and Guilds schemes introduced a practical and non-academic approach strongly advocated by the Institute.

A further important advance begun in 1988 was a review of City and Guilds' Senior Awards – the Fellowship (FCGI) and Associateship (ACGI), awarded by the Council exclusively to former students of City and Guilds College, Imperial College of Science and Technology, University of London; and the Insignia Award in Technology (CGIA) the origin of which in 1949 is described above. The aim was to re-establish a single, clear, progressive, industry-based structure leading on from City and Guilds specific vocational preparation qualifications – especially the Licentiateship introduced at the top of the new Certificates and Awards "ladder" adopted in 1978. In so doing, the Institute would once more provide its original span of qualifications from "Apprentices, Workmen, Foremen, Managers, to Principals of Manufactories." In contemporary terms this meant from school students comparable to those aged 14-17 originally attending the full-time day classes at Finsbury, through trainees and entrants to employment, skilled and competent workpeople, supervisors, to managers at the equivalent of graduate and professional levels. All the City and Guilds Senior Awards concerned carried postnominal designatory letters authorised by H M Privy Council through the Institute's Instruments of Governance, and the outcome of the review would require Privy Council approval for any changes.

The continued growth of the Institute's operations made necessary the acquisition of additional accommodation. After thorough search which showed it was not possible to secure suitable premises adjacent to either 76 Portland Place or 46 Britannia Street, a long lease of Nos. 320-326 City Road, London, EC1, refurbished to a high standard, was taken. This expansion provided the opportunity to instal a new telephone and data transmission system linking the Institute's three sets of premises, and to expand the micro-computer network (see above).

The theme of the Report for 1989-90 was "Qualifications to Achieve". The Chairman of Council, Mr H M Neal, stated: "More City and Guilds qualifications are accredited for award as National Vocational Qualifications than those of any other body. City and Guilds regards this as an important public contribution to the national aim of improving the numbers and standards of skilled people in the community. The new specifications of assessments for qualifications in new occupational fields, and the redevelopment of existing qualifications, have all been provided out of City and Guilds' own resources and at no extra cost to public funds." The Director-General in his Review of the year's work, after recording the financial surplus on the year's operations, described the new Senior Awards structure approved by the Council in July 1990 as "a great step forward in the provision of relevant, valid qualifications."

The Council, meeting in Founders' Hall, resolved to amend the Institute's Statutes and Standing Orders and to submit the amendments to H M Privy Council to be formally allowed, so as to provide with effect from 1 October 1990 a new structure of awards leading to the highest levels of professional practice. The characteristics of the new structure were that it was (a) comprehensive to all technologies and professional activities recognised and provided for by the Institute, (b) progressive from award upward to award, or accessible laterally, (c) accessible, open to anyone who can fulfil the requirements and meet the necessary standards, and (d) competence-based, on the demonstration of the practical application of professional skills, knowledge and understanding.

The new awards, above the Career Extension stage of the existing Certificates and Awards structure, were Licentiateship (LCGI); Graduateship (GCGI) – to which the existing Associateship (ACGI), retained for graduates of City and Guilds College only, is equivalent in level; Membership (MCGI) – by qualification, superseding the Insignia Award in Technology (CGIA); and Fellowship (FCGI) – at the existing level of professional excellence, but no longer exclusively in Engineering and to former students of City and Guilds College. Detailed Regulations for each award were drawn up, setting out the criteria and procedures to be followed. An important advance was provision for the Institute to delegate authority to conduct assessments, subject to the final conferment of awards by the Council, to universities, polytechnics, training establishments, professional institutions and major employers. This built upon the procedures long established in the case of City and Guilds College, and evolved with the Royal Military College of Science and the Royal Naval Engineering College.

To carry forward the Institute's concern with maintaining the highest standards of practical craftsmanship, it also introduced the annual award of the City and Guilds Gold Medal for Craft Excellence, for an outstanding workpiece designed and made by the recipient. Candidates might be from any aspect of technology and must hold a City and Guilds qualification. The first Gold Medal was presented to Dr Graham White of Sheffield University for a cast gold alloy dental beam supported by "Branemark" implants: the award was made at the Yearly Meeting on 8 March 1990 in Clothworkers' Hall by the Rt Hon The Lord Mayor of London, Sir Hugh Bidwell.

The year 1989-90 was highly successful for City and Guilds, as the result of increasingly effective forward planning in previous years. All aspects of operational and financial planning had become fully integrated and effectively controlled, so that the Institute's approach was as proactive as it could be in the prevailing education and training environment – which the Institute was able to evaluate with increasing success due to its increasingly wide range of positive contacts. Close co-operation was being maintained with the Confederation of British Industry (CBI); with NCVQ; with SEAC; and with the Engineering Council, which this year accorded recognition to LCGI in certain Engineering applications for registration as an Engineering Technician (EngTech). City and Guilds mounted a special initiative to establish positive relationships with the new Training and Enterprise Councils (TECs), established by the Department of Employment on a local basis to plan and co-ordinate employers' personnel and training requirements with resources available in the area. The TECs comprised industrialists and educationalists, and City and Guilds organised a series of regional conferences for members at which Institute members and staff gave presentations and informal briefings. Also with the aim of maintaining and extending cordial relationships with key figures in industry and business, education and training, central and local government, and the City and Livery Companies, regular luncheons were held informally at 76 Portland Place at which the Chairman of Council and Honorary Officers, Director-General and senior staff acted as hosts. Still with the same objective of improving sources of information and advice, a major reconstitution of City and Guilds' National Advisory Committee structure and memberships was put in hand, in which the committees were related to the current sectors of industry and the members were predominantly drawn from industry. Educationalists and trainers predominated in the membership of the Examination Subject Committees by which detailed objectives, content, and criteria for City and Guilds qualifications continued to be defined and stated.

The system of collaborative Agreements with other organisations in order to advance shared interests was further expanded: one of the significant organisations to be included was Foras Aiseanna Saothair (FAS), the Republic of Ireland Training and Employment Authority, with which the Director-General signed the Agreement for joint testing and certification in Dublin in April 1990.

The progressively better alignment between City and Guilds' services and the State system of education and training was further demonstrated in the Prime Minister, John Major's, statement on 3 July 1991 affirming his and his Government's belief in the necessity for rigour in the moderation and assessment of standards, and for parity of public esteem as between vocational and academic educational qualifications – principles which City and Guilds had been advocating from its foundation.

The Institute's year 1990-91 must be accounted one of its most successful and probably the most successful overall of its history to date. City and Guilds' services were provided to a greater number of people than ever before. For the first time since its original plan was given effect in the 1880s, the Institute was able through its awards structure to provide a complete "ladder" of opportunity and progression from age 14 to the highest levels of professional practice, with qualifications at each industrially-recognised level of employment. The structure comprised three main stages. The first stage was the new, Government-approved City and Guilds Diploma of Vocational Education at Foundation Level (14-16), Intermediate and National Levels (16-19), progressively subsuming the previous Foundation Programmes and CPVE, from the joint administration of which it was agreed at meetings of the parties concerned with Mr Tim Eggar, Minister of State for Education and Science, held in December 1990 and June 1991, BTEC would withdraw by 30 September 1991. The second stage was the City and Guilds Certificates of specific vocational preparation at Levels 1, 2 and 3 and at Career Extension Level, complementary to training and experience after leaving school and many of them accredited as NVQs at the relevant levels. The third stage was the Senior Awards, described above. As the Director-General, John Barnes, wrote: "The existence of a coherent, progressive and comprehensive structure of City and Guilds qualifications, related to employment levels and in many cases accredited as National Vocational Qualifications (NVQ), will make it easier for students, parents, teachers and trainers, careers advisers and employers, to evaluate City and Guilds certificates and diplomas correctly and to gain maximum benefit from their possession and use."

The Government's White Paper, *Education and Training for the 21st Century*, published in May 1991, contained proposals welcomed by the Institute in all those respects in which they concerned City and Guilds' activities: it was particularly encouraging to find that most of the White Paper's aims for the future qualifications system, especially those of removing barriers and of enhancing the active involvement of employers, were already addressed in the Institute's Corporate Plan for 1991-96.

In December 1990 City and Guilds extended its range of measurement and qualification services into the complementary field of office and secretarial qualifications by the purchase of the Pitman Examinations Institute (PEI). PEI was particularly strong overseas and its overseas administrative structure formed a valuable enhancement to City and Guilds' overseas operations. In the initial stages PEI continues to operate from its premises at Godalming, Surrey, as an autonomous division of City and Guilds for commercial and business subjects: the acquisition however represents a major advance in City and Guilds' provision and strengthens still further the Institute's position as a major independent body serving the public throughout the world.

At the highest level of the Institute, 1991-92 marked the Fortieth Anniversary of Her Majesty The Queen's succession to the Throne and consequently to the office of Visitor of the Institute in accordance with the Royal Charter of Incorporation. 1991 was also the Fortieth Anniversary of His Royal Highness The Duke of Edinburgh's acceptance of election as the Institute's President. In celebration of Prince Philip's commitment to City and Guilds throughout the 40 years of his Presidency to date, the Institute was privileged to present to him a special commemorative Gold Medal modelled on his own Prince Philip Medals. On behalf of the Institute the Chairman of Council presented the Medal to the President at a small luncheon at which the Honorary Officers, Director-General, and the Prince Philip Medallist for 1991 were present, following the Medals Presentation at Buckingham Palace, on 10 July 1991. The Medals Presentation was itself a significant development in that for the first time the President presented a representative selection of the Silver and Bronze Medals awarded for outstanding performance in the City and Guilds examinations of the previous year, as well as the Prince Philip Medal. One Silver and one Bronze Medal winner from each of the 10 Regions of England and Wales with whose Regional Advisory Council the Institute collaborates were selected by the Regional Council to receive his or her Medal from the Duke of Edinburgh. A similar pattern was followed at Buckingham Palace on 8 July 1992, when Medal Winners from Scotland and Northern Ireland were also included.

The Chairman of Council, Mr Paul Wates, introducing the Report for 1991-92 wrote: ". . . the Institute has enjoyed another extremely successful year in what by common consent from an economic standpoint has been one of the most difficult years in recent memory." The dominant themes of the year were the continuation of collaboration with NCVQ; consolidation of the City and Guilds' "ladder of progression" through qualifications; and international expansion.

The 100 000th NVQ to be awarded by City and Guilds – half the national total at the time – was presented at a special ceremony at 76 Portland Place on 31 July 1992. The Chairman of NCVQ, Sir Bryan Nicholson, writing in his Council's Annual Report for 1991-92, made special mention of City and Guilds' contribution to the establishment of the NVQ framework (in conjunction with industry and business Lead Bodies) over the previous six years. City and Guilds devoted increasing attention to the development and introduction of General National Vocational Qualifications (GNVQ) at Levels 2 and 3 for students opting to continue in full-time education at age 16: GNVQ provide alternatives (or complements) to four GCSEs at Level 2 and to two "A" levels at Level 3. The broadly-based GNVQ courses in Art and Design; Business; Health and Social Care; Leisure and Tourism; and Manufacturing, being pioneered at 90 colleges at the time of writing, have been to some extent developed on the basis of the City and Guilds Diploma of Vocational Education. They reflect the main areas of the British economy and of young people's interests, and were first proposed in the Government's White Paper, *Education and Training for the 21st Century*. This, and the White Paper *Choice and Diversity*, both re-emphasised the need for parity of esteem between vocational and academic qualifications.

In recognition of the identity of view between the Institute and the Government on the equal status of the vocational and the academic, the Council invited the Prime Minister, John Major, to accept the Institute's highest award, Honorary Fellowship (Hon FCGI). It was a source of gratification to City and Guilds that Mr Major accepted, and received the Diploma of Honorary Fellow from the Chairman of Council on 29 January 1992 at No. 10, Downing Street in the presence of Honorary Officers and the Director-General. The event "set the seal" on the comprehensive structure of City and Guilds qualifications introduced in 1990 and bringing the varied developments of the Institute's entire history into coherent relationship.

Internationally, City and Guilds' collaborative services extended more widely than ever before, into parts of the world hitherto closed by ideology. Working links were established with China; South Africa; and the United States of America and Canada (where the Institute set up an associated organisation, City and Guilds North America Inc, with offices in Westerville, Ohio). The European Community came to be regarded as a "Home" rather than "Overseas" sector for City and Guilds examinations and services, which developed especially with reference to competence in languages and Information Technology.

The Director-General, John Barnes (who announced in late 1992 that he would retire on 31 March 1993), writing in review of 1991-92 in the Report, referred particularly to three more "domestic" features of the Institute's year. Operationally, attention had been focused on the development and expansion of the assessment and certification of trainers, assessors, and verifiers of standards, to meet increasing concentration in all occupational sectors on reliable quality assurance systems to support the successful implementation of NVQs. Regionally, the interaction of the Institute throughout its history with Regional Examining Bodies and Advisory Councils entered an entirely new era of partnership with the completion of a further series of seven individual formal Agreements for the establishment of City and Guilds Teams in the Regional Organisations throughout England. The Teams are to undertake the functions of centre approval and monitoring, promotional and staff development work and local contacts with organisations including the Training and Enterprise Councils. Activities in Wales are conducted under an Agreement with the Welsh Joint Education Committee, and Scotland and Northern Ireland each has a City and Guilds Liaison Officer. Constitutionally, the Membership of the Institute of every one of the 100 Livery Companies of the City of London currently existing was achieved during 1991-92 – a most satisfying confirmation of the importance and value of the enterprise begun in the Mansion House 120 years before.

The 1991-92 Report, *Crediting Competence,* records an unprecedented number of 2 335 005 examination component or unit entries from home and overseas, reflecting both an increase over the previous year and the Institute's continuing move towards unit-based schemes.

During 1992 a Review of the City and Guilds of London Institute by Dr T P Melia, CBE, former Senior Chief Inspector, H M Inspectorate of Schools, was commissioned. The Review concludes: "The Institute enters 1993 on a sound footing and is well placed to take advantage of the many opportunities with which it will be presented over the next decade." Influences on the longer-term future are identified as including: – the Further and Higher Education Act, 1992; industrial, social and demographic trends, especially towards higher participation rates in further and higher education and the development of NVQ; implementation of the National Curriculum in schools, and its effects beyond age 16; the introduction of General National Vocational Qualifications (GNVQ); the national need for less-costly assessment procedures; opportunities internationally, especially in the USA and China; and growing demands for full-time further education and to provide for female candidates for City and Guilds examinations. This *Short History* describes the Institute's record of flexibility in providing for current

160

trends throughout 115 years: the record is an appropriate starting point for Dr Melia's concluding paragraph, which runs:-

"In approaching the future City and Guilds should not hide its light under a bushel. It is uniquely placed to give a lead on many vocational education and training issues. It is financially sound; it is independent; it is concerned with and about standards; it is flexible; it has a research and development arm unique amongst bodies of its type; it has close links with industry and commerce, training organisations and education; and its comprehensive and progressive awards structure should allow it to bring some sense and simplification into the education and training qualifications jungle."

Table 5 City and Guilds Staff numbers

1890 Head office   4 } 10
    Technological Exams   6 }
    Central Institution – Teaching   18
                 Admin   4
    Finsbury College   – Teaching   25
                 Admin   4
    Art School   – Teaching   7
                 Admin   3   Total 71

1900 Head Office   4 } 13
    Technological Exams   9 }
    Central Technical College   40
    Finsbury College   44
    Art School   8   Total 105

1910 Head Office   4 } 16
    Technological Exams   12 }
    City and Guilds College   66
    Finsbury College   48
    Art School   8   Total 138

1920 Head Office   4 } 16
    Technological Exams   12 }
    C&G College Delegacy: *not published*
    Finsbury College   42
    Art School   8   Total 66

1930 Head Office   3 } 18
    Technological Exams   15 }
    C&G College *N/A*
    Finsbury College: *closed*
    Art School   8   Total 26

1934 Head Office   3 } 23
    Dept of Technology   20 }   Total 23

1939   Department of Technology   39 (total Institute)

1949   Department of Technology   90 (total Institute)

Table 5 City and Guilds Staff numbers (contd)

1952	Head Office and Department of Technology	86
1953	Head Office and Department of Technology	96
1954	Head Office and Department of Technology	109
1955	Head Office and Department of Technology (Art School 14)	96
1956	Head Office and Department of Technology (Art School 14)	126
1957	Head Office and Department of Technology (Art School 14)	127
1958	Head Office (AEB included) (Art School 14)	137
1959	Head Office (AEB included) (Art School 16)	131
1960	Head Office (AEB included) (Art School 13)	149
1961	Head Office (AEB included) (Art School 13)	158
1962	Head Office (AEB included) (Art School 13)	175
1963	Head Office (AEB included) (Art School 13)	182
1964	Head Office (AEB included) (Art School 13)	217
1965	Head Office (AEB included) (Art School 14)	217
1966	Head Office (AEB included) (Art School 16)	261
1967	Head Office (Art School 15)	227
1976		380
1977		400
1979		437
1980		430
1981		393
1982		327
1983		334
1984		360
1985		360

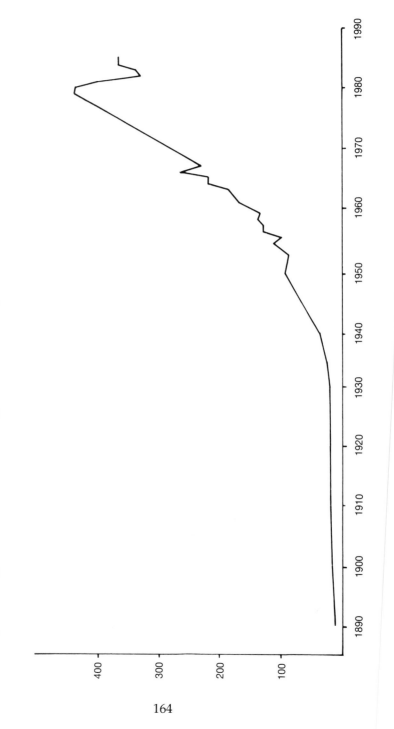

City and Guilds of London Institute Staff: Head Office and Department of Technology (including Associated Examining Board 1958-66)

Institute Premises

Headquarters

1879-80	Mercers' Hall, London, EC
1881-1913	Gresham College, London, EC
1913	3 St Helen's Place, London, EC – during re-building of Gresham College
1914	Leonard Street, London, EC (City and Guilds Finsbury Technical College) – during re-building of Gresham College
1915-57	Gresham College, Basinghall Street, London, EC
1958-	76 Portland Place, London, W1

Technological Examinations

1879-80	Mercers' Hall, London, EC
1881-87	Gresham College, London, EC
1887-91	City and Guilds of London Central Institution, South Kensington

Examinations Department

1891-1903	Exhibition Road (Royal School of Needlework), South Kensington

Department of Technology (to 1956)

1903-22	Exhibition Road, London, SW
1923-31	29 Roland Gardens, South Kensington, London, SW
1931-58	31 Brechin Place, London, SW7
1958-	76 Portland Place, London, W1

Examinations Department (and others)

1974-	46 Britannia Street, London, WC1

Curriculum, Test Development and Research Department (and others)

1989-	326 City Road, London, EC1

Pitman Examinations Institute

1990-	Catteshall Manor, Godalming, Surrey, GU7 1UU

City and Guilds Technical College, Finsbury
1881-1926   Leonard Street, London, EC

South London Technical Art School
1879-1932   122-124 Kennington Park Road, London, SE

City and Guilds of London Institute Kennington and Lambeth Art School
1932-37   118-124 Kennington Park Road, London, SE
                (freeholds of 118-120 acquired by the Institute in 1933)

City and Guilds of London Art School
1937-71   118-124 Kennington Park Road, London, SE
                (with effect from 1 April 1971 the Institute made a gift of
                these freehold premises to the City and Guilds of London
                Art School Limited)

Central Institution
1884-93   Exhibition Road, London, SW

Central Technical College
1893-1910   Exhibition Road, London, SW

City and Guilds College
1911-62   Imperial College of Science and Technology, South Kensington,
                London, SW7
                (the Institute's original leasehold premises and building dating from
                1881 were transferred to the Delegacy of the City and Guilds College
                with effect from 1 January 1911 and on the demolition of the building
                during the redevelopment of Imperial College in 1962 the Institute's
                interest in this asset was finally extinguished).

The Visitors of the City and Guilds of London Institute

by authority of the Royal Charter of Incorporation, 26 October 1900

1900-01	Her Majesty Queen Victoria
1901-10	His Majesty King Edward VII – also Patron
1910-36	His Majesty King George V
1936	His Majesty King Edward VIII
1936-52	His Majesty King George VI
1952-	Her Majesty Queen Elizabeth II

The Presidents of the Institute

by authority of the Memorandum and Articles of Association, 6 July 1880

1881-1900   His Royal Highness Albert Edward, Prince of Wales, KG, Mercer

by authority of the Royal Charter of Incorporation, 26 October 1900

1900-01   His Royal Highness Albert Edward, Prince of Wales, KG, Mercer
1951-   His Royal Highness The Duke of Edinburgh, KG, KT, Fishmonger

The Vice-Presidents of the Institute

by authority of the Memorandum and Articles of Association, 6 July 1880

1882-95	The Earl of Selborne, FRS, Mercer
1882-1903	*Sir Frederick Bramwell, Bart., FRS, Goldsmith
1882-1906	*Sir Sydney Waterlow, Bart., KCVO, Alderman, MP, Clothworker
1885-91	Sir Robert Fowler, Bart., Alderman, MP, Salter
1889-93	Herbert C Saunders, QC, Skinner
1892-93	Daniel Watney, Mercer
1892-1907	*Henry Hucks Gibbs, Lord Aldenham
1894-1903	*Edward Lonsdale Beckwith, Fishmonger
1896-1920	*The Earl of Halsbury, FRS, Saddler

by authority of the Royal Charter of Incorporation, 26 October 1900 (in which those marked * above are named as the first Vice-Presidents under the Charter)

1904-09	S Steuart Gladstone, JP, Fishmonger
1904-17	Sir John Wolfe-Barry, KCB, FRS, Goldsmith
1910-12	George Baker, Merchant Taylor
1913-15	J A Travers, Fishmonger
1916-25	Sir Edward Busk, Fishmonger
1918-25	L B Sebastian, Skinner
1921-22	Sir John Watney, Mercer
1925-45	T Savile Watney, ACGI, Mercer
1926-31	Morton Latham, JP, DL, Clothworker
1926-38	J R Drake, Grocer
1927-53	Sir Henry Steward, TD, Skinner
1932-38	Sir William Pope, KBE, FCGI, FRS, Goldsmith
1939-69	Professor R S Hutton, Goldsmith
1939-57	Walter T Prideaux, Goldsmith
1946-48	Brigadier H Clementi Smith, DSO, Mercer
1949-61	Sir Frederick Handley Page, CBE, FCGI, Coachmaker
1949	Walter A Prideaux, CBE, MC, TD, Goldsmith
1950	Sir George Aylwen, Bart., Alderman, Merchant Taylor
1954-56	Hon Maurice Lubbock, Fishmonger

1954-55	Major Walter F Pothecary, DCM, JP, Clothworker
1958-71	Brigadier-General Sir Harold Hartley, CH, GCVO, CBE, MC, FRS, Goldsmith
1958-69	Arthur Montague Holbein, CBE, FCGI, Ironmonger
1958-61	Lord Nelson of Stafford, FCGI, Goldsmith
1960-67	Colonel A T Maxwell, TD, Mercer
1967-73	Sir Graham Savage, CB
1969-77	Lord Penney, OM, KBE, FRS
1971-84	Lord Robens of Woldingham, PC
1971-77	Sir Joseph Hunt, MBE
1972-81	Sir William Ryland, CB
1975-79	Sir Denis Barnes, KCB
1976-78	Lady Plowden, DBE
1978-80	Sir Eric Richardson, CBE
1979-83	Dame Kathleen Ollerenshaw, DBE, DL
1979 for life	Sir David Woodbine Parish, CBE, Hon FCGI, Clothworker
1981-90	Sir Alex Smith
1982-92	Sir William Barlow, FEng, Engineer
1983-	Lord Chapple of Hoxton
1984-	Lord Gregson of Stockport, DL
1985-89	Sir Stanley Grinstead, Brewer
1990-	Lord King of Wartnaby, Hon FCGI
1991-	The Earl of Selborne, KBE, DL, Mercer
1992-	Sir Clifford Chetwood, Hon FCGI, Basketmaker

The Chairmen of Council

1878-95	The Earl of Selborne, FRS, Mercer
1896-1920	The Earl of Halsbury, FRS, Saddler
1921-23	Sir John Watney, Mercer
1925	Sir Edward Busk, Fishmonger
1926-31	Morton Latham, JP, DL, Clothworker
1932-38	Sir William Pope, KBE, FCGI, FRS, Goldsmith
1939-48	Professor R S Hutton, Goldsmith
1949-61	Sir Frederick Handley Page, CBE, FCGI, Coachmaker
1962-66	Arthur Montague Holbein, CBE, FCGI, Ironmonger
1967-79	Sir David Woodbine Parish, CBE, Hon FCGI, Clothworker
1979-91	H Morton Neal, CBE, FCGI, FIC, Carpenter
1991-	Paul C R Wates, Clothworker

The Chairmen of the Executive Committee

1878-89	Sir Frederick Bramwell, Bart., FRS, Goldsmith
1889-93	Herbert C Saunders, QC, Skinner
1894-1902	Sir Frederick Abel, Bart., GCVO, KCB, FRS, Goldsmith
1903-17	Sir John Wolfe-Barry, KCB, FRS, Goldsmith
1918-24	Major Sir Edward Busk, Fishmonger
1925-45	T Savile Watney, ACGI, Mercer
1946-48	Brigadier H Clementi Smith, DSO, Mercer
1949-61	Sir Frederick Handley Page, CBE, FCGI, Coachmaker
1962-66	Arthur Montague Holbein, CBE, FCGI, Ironmonger
1967-78	Sir David Woodbine Parish, CBE, Hon FCGI, Clothworker
1978-91	H Morton Neal, CBE, FCGI, FIC, Carpenter
1991-	Paul C R Wates, Clothworker

The Joint Honorary Secretaries of the Institute

1878-1920	Sir John Watney, Clerk, Mercers' Company
1878-87	Sir William Phillips Sawyer, Clerk, Drapers' Company
1878-86	Sir Owen Roberts, Clerk, Clothworkers' Company
1889-90	Walter Prideaux, Clerk, Goldsmiths' Company
1911-18	S W Luard, Salter
1916-18	Walter T Prideaux, Goldsmith
1919-43	Peter MacIntyre Evans, CBE, Clerk, Clothworker's Company
1941-51	Major Walter F Pothecary, DCM, JP, Clerk, Clothworker's Company
1948-54	John Edward Coomber, Clerk, Clothworkers' Company
1952-59	H C Osborne, MC, Carpenter
1955-66	Sir David Woodbine Parish, CBE, Hon FCGI, Clothworker
1960-68	W R Nichols, TD, Clerk, Salters' Company
1966-69	S E Goodall, CBE
1969-74	P S Palmer, Mercer
1970-77	Sir Eric Richardson, CBE
1974-76	H Morton Neal, CBE, FCGI, FIC, Carpenter
1977-86	G H Jolly, MBE, TD
1978-85	D E Mumford, CBE
1986-	M G Venn, CBE
1987-90	Paul C R Wates, Clothworker
1991-	F K Chorley, CBE, FEng, Scientific Instrument Maker

The Treasurers of the Institute

1878-91	Sir Sydney Waterlow, Bart., KCVO, Alderman, MP, Clothworker
1892-93	Daniel Watney, Mercer
1894-1902	Edward Lonsdale Beckwith, Fishmonger
1903-09	S Steuart Gladstone, Fishmonger
1910-12	George Baker, Merchant Taylor
1913-15	J A Travers, Fishmonger
1916-17	Sir Edward Busk, Fishmonger
1918-25	L B Sebastian, Skinner
1926-38	J R Drake, Grocer
1939-49	Walter T Prideaux, Goldsmith
1949	Walter A Prideaux, CBE, MC, TD, Goldsmith
1950	Sir George Aylwen, Bart., Alderman, Merchant Taylor
1954-56	Hon. Maurice Lubbock, Fishmonger
1959-66	Colonel A T Maxwell, TD, Mercer
1967-77	J F Shearer, CBE
1978-81	D M Clement, CBE
1982-89	R N D Langdon
1990-	J Ian Andrew, Carman and Chartered Accountant

Chairmen of Examinations Committee

1895-1903   George Matthey FRS, Goldsmith

Technology Committee

1903-04   George Matthey FRS, Goldsmith
1905-06   William Bousfield, Clothworker
1907-10   Sir William Bousfield, Clothworker
1911-32   Morton Latham, Clothworker
1933-47   Sir Henry Steward, Skinner
1948-49   A Montague Holbein, Ironmonger
1950-59   A Montague Holbein, CBE, FCGI, Ironmonger

Educational Policy Committee

1959-64   A Montague Holbein, CBE, FCGI, Ironmonger
1965-67   Sir Graham Savage, CB

Policy Committee for Education and Training

1967-70   Sir Graham Savage, CB
1970-80   Sir Eric Richardson, CBE
1981-85   Deryck E Mumford, CBE
1986-   Maurice G Venn, CBE

The Chief Officers of the Institute

Director and Secretary

1880-88   Philip Magnus

Educational Adviser

1888-90   Sir Philip Magnus

Superintendent of Technological Examinations

1891-1901   Sir Philip Magnus

Superintendent of the Department of Technology

1902-15   Sir Philip Magnus, MP
1916-21   Leonard G Killby
1922-35   Charles C Hawkins, CBE
1936-49   Lieut. Colonel William French, CBE, DSO, MC

Administrative Director, later Director, Department of Techology, and Director of the Institute

1949-62   Major-General Cyril Lloyd, CB, CBE, TD

Director-General

1962-67   Major-General Cyril Lloyd, CB, CBE, TD
1968-76   Sir Cyril English
1976-85   Major-General Harry Knutton, CB
1985-93   John A Barnes, CBE

Unpublished Sources

1 *City of London Guildhall Library (Department of Manuscripts)*

Minutes of Lord Mayor's preliminary meetings 1872-73   Ms 22 000

Institute Archives 1876-1967 (fully catalogued)   Ms 21 810-999

2 *City and Guilds of London Institute, 76 Portland Place, London, W1N 4AA*

Programmes of Regulations and Syllabuses for Technological Examinations 1880 – date (some omissions)

Miscellaneous archive materials

F E Foden, *A History of Technical Examinations in England to 1918: with Special Reference to the Examination Work of the City and Guilds of London Institute* (unpublished PhD thesis, University of Reading, 1961)

3 *Public Record Office, Kew*

Board of Education/Ministry of Education/ Department of Education and Science Records   Ed 46

Ed 46 7	Untitled but refers to Institute, 1904-35
Ed 46 156	City and Guilds of London Institute, 1936-44
Ed 46 370	City and Guilds of London Institute, 1945-47
Ed 46 856	City and Guilds of London Institute, 1962
Ed 46 863	"Concordat", 1968

Bibliography

A **The Institute generally, and its Technological Examinations**

Jennifer Lang, *City and Guilds of London Institute Centenary 1878-1978: an Historical Commentary* (London, City and Guilds of London Institute, 1978)

Frank Foden, *Philip Magnus: Victorian Educational Pioneer* (London, Vallentine, Mitchell, 1970)

Philip Magnus, *Educational Aims and Efforts, 1880-1910* (London, Longmans, 1911)

R S Hutton, *Recollections of a Technologist* (London, Pitman, 1964)

C T Millis, *Technical Education: its Development and Aims* (London, Edward Arnold, 1925)

Victor Belcher, *The City Parochial Foundation 1891-1991: a Trust for the Poor of London* (Scolar Press, Aldershot, 1991)

Derek Hudson and Kenneth W Luckhurst, *The Royal Society of Arts, 1754-1954* (London, John Murray, 1954)

G A N Lowndes, *The Silent Social Revolution: an Account of the Expansion of Public Education in England and Wales 1895-1935* (London, Oxford University Press, 1937)

Michael Argles, *South Kensington to Robbins: an Account of English Technical and Scientific Education since 1851* (London, Longmans, 1964)

John Charles Thornley and George W Hastings (eds), *The Guilds of the City of London and their Liverymen* (London, The London and Counties Press Association, Limited, c.1911)

Colin R Chapman, *The Growth of British Education and its Records* (Lochin Publishing, Dursley, 1991)

B **City and Guilds Finsbury Technical College**

J Vargas Eyre, *Henry Edward Armstrong, 1848-1937: The Doyen of British Chemists and Pioneer of Technical Education* (London, Butterworths, 1958)

C **City and Guilds Central Institution/Central Technical College/College**

Adrian Whitworth (ed), *City and Guilds College, 1885-1985: a Centenary History* (London, City and Guilds College of Imperial College of Science and Technology, 1985)

Joyce Brown (ed), *A Hundred Years of Civil Engineering at South Kensington: The Origins and History of the Department of Civil Engineering of Imperial College, 1884-1984* (London, Civil Engineering Department, Imperial College, 1985)

E G Walker, *The Life and Work of William Cawthorne Unwin* (London, George Allen and Unwin, 1947)

A Rupert Hall, *Science for Industry: a Short History of The Imperial College of Science and Technology* (London, Imperial College, 1982)

D **The Associated Examining Board**

H G Earnshaw, *The Associated Examining Board for the General Certificate of Education: Origin and History* (The Associated Examining Board, Aldershot, 1974)

E **City and Guilds Provision for Part-Time Teachers**

Frank Foden, *The Education of Part-Time Teachers in Further and Adult Education: a Retrospective Study* (University of Leeds, Leeds Studies in Continuing Education, 1992)

F **The Prince Philip Medal**

City and Guilds of London Institute, *The Prince Philip Medal: The Medal, its purpose, and the Prince Philip Medallists 1962-89* (London, City and Guilds of London Institute, 1989)

G **City and Guilds and the Royal Family**

City and Guilds of London Institute, *The Royal Family and the Institute* (London, City and Guilds of London Institute, 1993)

Index

A Basis for Choice 131
A Better Start in Working Life 131
A Review of the Examination System of the City and Guilds of London Institute
by J L Brereton 91
Accreditation of Prior Learning (APL)150-151
Accredited Centres for Skills Testing, Institute's 136
Act, Board of Education, 1899 50 54
Act, Education, 1902 53 55
Act, Education, 1918 62-63
Act, Education, 1944 61 84 88 115 127
Act, Education Reform 1988 151
Act, Employment and Training, 1973 135
Act, Further and Higher Education, 1992 160
Act, Industrial Training, 1964 66 104 112 115 118
Act, Local Taxation, 1890 46-47
Act, Technical Instruction, 1889 35 46
Administrative Memoranda, DES/SED 119 120
Advisory Committees, Institute's 52 65 68 70-74 81-83 89 95 120
Agreements, Collaborative 145-146 148 150-151 155 159
Agricultural Education 146
Albany, HRH The Duke of (1853-84) 31
Anderson, Sir William 15
Appeal to Industry 96 98 100-101
Apprenticeship 11 15 120
Armourers and Brasiers' Company 17 20
Armstrong, Lord 17
"Ashby" Commission on Higher Education in Nigeria 109
Associated Examining Board (AEB) 96 107 110
Associated Electrical Industries (AEI) 102

Association of British Travel Agents (ABTA) 134
Association of Education Committees 69
Association of Organising Secretaries 54
Association of Principals of Technical Institutions 80 107
Association of Teachers in Technical Institutions 79-81 107
Association of Technical Institutions 52 54 66 80 108
Australia 85

Baker, Kenneth 147 149
Barnes, John 139 145 149 156 159
Bartley, Sir George 17
"Beloe" Report 107 129
Better Opportunities in Technical Education, White Paper 1961 94 109 111
Bidwell, Sir Hugh 154
Birmingham, Municipal Technical School 47
Board of Education 50 53-62 64-69 71-72 74-76 78 83-85 88
Bombay, India 48
Bousfield, Sir William 46
Bramwell, Sir Frederick 17 20-21 30 36
Bristol, Merchant Venturers' School 47
British Aerospace (BAe) 140
British Association for Commercial and Industrial Education 109
British Computer Society 116
British Guiana and West Indies 85
British Red Cross Society 82
Broadsheet, Institute's 101 127
"Brunton" Report 113
Buckingham Palace 157
Budget, Institute (also Finance) 19 22 31-33 56 64 80 90 92 96-97 101 103 123 126 129 151
Burma 85
Business and Technician (Technology) Education Council (BTEC) 59 131 142 145-146 149
Business Education Council (BEC) 59 111 125-128 131 141-142 149

Busk, Sir Edward 66
Butler, Rt Hon R A 83-84
Butten, E E 92

Callaghan, James 130
Canada 85
Carnarvon, Earl of 15
Carpenters' Company 20
Centenary, Institute's 136-138
Central Institution, City and Guilds (see also Central Technical College; City and Guilds College) 18 22 30-31 34 36
Central Technical College, City and Guilds 49 53 55 57
Central Training Council 112
Centres for Examinations, Institute's 27 29 78 117
Certificate of Pre-Vocational Education (CPVE) 131 147 149
Certificates 19 25 29 34 46 48 54 79 88 94 117 127 141 156
Certificates of Travel Agency Competence (COTAC) 134
Ceylon 85
Chandos, Viscount 102
Charity Commissioners 36
Chester, County Hall 110
Choice and Diversity, White Paper 158
City and Guilds College 58 63 79 101 137 151 153
City and Guilds Diploma in Technology/ Insignia Award in Technology 92 151 153
City and Guilds of London Institute 11 19-20 66 68 80 100 122 146
City and Guilds Insignia Award Association 120
City and Guilds: the Next Five Years, 1988-1993 149
City and Guilds North America Inc 159
City and Guilds of London Art School 99 101 124
City and Guilds Ordinary and Higher Technician Diplomas 99
City of London 12 30 78 96 102
City Parochial Charities (London) 36
Clothworkers' Company 12 16-17 20 47 49 60

Clothworkers' Hall 154
Coachmakers' Company 14
Cole, Sir Henry 14
Commissioners of Exhibition of 1851 15 30
Committee for Industrial Training, Institute's 122
Committee for Technical Education, Institute's 121
Committee for Work Overseas, Institute's 99 123
Commonwealth Technical Training Week 106 109 111
Communication Skills and Numeracy 134
Competence-based approach 143
Computer Education 116
Computer processing of examinations 116 138-139
"Concordat" Agreement 99 109
Confederation of British Industry (CBI) 130 140 154
Conference of Educational Bodies on Technical Examinations for Students Attending Minor Courses in England and Wales 66 68
Conference of representatives of Local Education Authorities, Teachers and Examining Bodies 68
Consultative Committees, Institute's 95 98
Coopers' Company 20
Cordwainers' Company 17 20 49
Corporation of London 11 13 17 20 31 35 56 78 90 92 96 144
Council for National Academic Awards 90 101 115
Council of Technical Examining Bodies 110 123 140 149
Council of the Institute 19 29 32 34-35 69 83 88 115 121-126 129 133 138 141 144 148 150 153 158
County Councils Association 69
Craft Courses 104
Credit Accumulation 148 150-151
Crosland, Anthony 121
"Crowther" Report 107 129

Day-release 103 127
Delegacy of the City and Guilds College 58 72 89 124
Department of Education and Science (DES) 118-119 124 131 134 145 151
Department of Employment 126 132 145 154
Department of Employment and Productivity 132
Department of Technical Co– operation 109
Department of Technical Education and Agriculture, Ireland 53
Department of Technology, City and Guilds 49 55-57 65 70 72 78 81-82 88-89 91-94 97
Department of Trade and Industry (DTI) 140
Departmental Committee on examinations for part-time students in Technical Colleges and Schools 69
Departments, Institute's 110 117 126
Diploma of Vocational Education, City and Guilds 156
Director-General, Institute's 110
Donnelly, Major General Sir John 17 21
Douglas-Home, Sir Alec 113
Downing Street, No. 10 158
Drapers' Company 16-17 20 33
Drapers' Hall 17 22
Duke of Edinburgh, HRH The Prince Philip 95 101 110-111 122 137-138 157
Dyers' Company 20

East Africa 85
East Midland Educational Union (EMEU) 71 75 110
Eaton, Cecil 75
Eccles, Sir David 100
Eckersley, Tom 136
Education 76
Education: A Framework for Expansion, White Paper 127
Education and Training for the 21st Century, White Paper 156 158
Education and Training of 16-18 Year Olds 131

Education for the Printing Industry. . . 112
Education in Schools, Green Paper 130
Educational Policy Committee, Institute's 94 111-112 115 119 121
Educational Testing Service, Princeton, NJ, USA 123
Eggar, Tim 156
Egypt 85
Engineering Council 154
Engineering ITB 119 123 135
Engineering, Royal Academy (Fellowship) of 138
English, Sir Cyril 106 121
English-Speaking Union 79
Entry Fees 34 93 101
European Economic Community (EEC) 109 128 150 159
Evans, P M 83
Examination Structures and Procedures 127
Examination Subject Committees 155
Examination Techniques 91
Examination Techniques Development Unit (ETDU) 123 127
Examinations at 17 plus 131
Examinations Board, Institute's 24 60 65 75 80 83 121
Examinations Committee (see also Technology Committee) 24 46
Examinations, Final 67 78-80
Examinations, Intermediate 67 74 78 80
Examinations, Practical 25 32 48 50 91 105
Examinations, Preliminary 48-49 58
Examinations, Technological 19 21-22 24 27-29 31-35 46-48 57-58 61-62 64 107 116
Examiners 23-24 50 89 117 122
Executive Committee of the Institute 17-22 47 64 89 99 115 121 125 141
Exhibitions 13 48 55 72 103 137
Exploratory Committees, Institute's 79

Fellowships, Honorary (Hon FCGI) 79 158
"Ferryside" Agreement 140 142
Finsbury Technical College, City and Guilds 22 31 34 36 50 55 63
Fishmongers' Company 17 20 137
Foras Aiseanna Saothair (FAS) 155

Foss, Mrs Olive 123
Foundation Courses, City and Guilds 129-131
Foundation Programmes, 14-16 131
Founders' Hall 153
French, Lt Col W 83
Full Technological Certificate (FTC) 23-24 29 49 58 73 98 125
Further Education Curriculum Review and Development Unit (FEU) 131
Further Education for Craftsmen 112
Further Education for Operatives 112
Further Education for Technicians 112
Further Education Staff College (Coombe Lodge) Blagdon 128

Galton, Sir Douglas 18
General Abilities Profile 146
General Employment Award, City and Guilds 134
General ("G") Courses 108
General National Vocational Qualifications (GNVQ) 132 158
General Regulations, Institute's 72
Gibraltar 85
Gladstone, W E 16 35
Gold Medal for Craft Excellence, City and Guilds 154
Goldsmiths' Company 17 20
Goldsmiths' Hall 22
Gorst, Sir John 50
Government Committees 69
Government Training Centres (GTCs) 132
Governors of the Institute 19 32
Grant of Coat-of-Arms 99
Great Exhibition of 1851 12
Gresham College 13 22
Grocers' Hall 95 101
Guildhall, City of London 102 137

H M Forces 127 144
H M Inspectors of Schools 73
H M The Queen 157
Haldane, Viscount 59
Halsbury, Earl of 56
Handley Page, Sir Frederick 93 95-96 100

"Haslegrave" Committee/Report 121-124 126 129 141
Headquarters, Institute's (76 Portland Place, London, W1) 98 101 105 126 153-154 157-158
Heath, Edward 124
"Henniker-Heaton" Report 113
Higher Education – Meeting the Challenge, White Paper 148
Higher (Technical) Education 85 88 90 94-95 148
Hills, Seymour, Director, Work Study School, Cranfield College of Aeronautics 105
Holbein, A M 121
Horsbrugh, Florence 95
House of Commons 50 125
Hughes, Thomas (1822-96) 12
Hutton, Professor R S 83-85 89 113
Huxley, Professor Thomas 18

Imperial College of Science and Technology 57 69 72 76 97 99
In-course Assessment 125 130
India 85
Industrial training: Government Proposals, White Paper 1963 111
Industry Lead Bodies 147 151 158
Industry, Participation of 96 98 100 128 144
Industry Training Boards (ITBs) 111 115 119 120 122 145
"Industry Year" 1986 147
Information Technology (IT) 146-148
Inspection of Classes (by Institute) 47 49 60
Institute of British Foundrymen 73
Institute of Training Development 147
Institution of Electrical Engineers 79
Institution of Heating and Ventilating Engineers 79
International Apprentice Competition 120 124
International Exhibition, Paris, 1900 53
International Youth Skill Olympics 150
Iraq 85
Ironmongers' Company 17 20

Jamaica 50
Job Training Scheme (JTS) 148
Joint Advisory Committees of City and
  Guilds and Regional Examining Bodies
  120 143
Joint Board for Pre-Vocational Education
  131 149-150
Joseph, Sir Keith 135

"Keir" Committee on Higher Education
  in Northern Rhodesia 109
Killby, Leonard G 59
King's College, London 22 33
Knutton, Harry 133

Lang, Jennifer 136
Latham, Morton 66
Leathersellers' Company 20
Liaison Officers, City and Guilds,
  Scotland; Northern Ireland 159
Liberal (General) Studies 98 104
Livery Companies 11-13 15 31 35 56 73 78
  80 90 92 95-96 100 144 145 160
Livery Companies' General Committee
  17-18 20
Livery Halls 14
Lloyd, Major-General Cyril 93 110 112
  121
Local Committees, Institute's 24-25
Local (Education) Authorities (LEA) 46
  53-54 57 64 66-69 75 78 88 93 108 119 130
  133
Local Secretaries, Institute's 25
London and Home Counties Regional
  Advisory Council 98
London Chamber of Commerce and
  Industry (LCCI) 145
London County Council 47 50 55-56 63
London School Board 33
Lord Mayor of London 12-13 15 59 72 92
  95-96 100 102 106 138
Lord Mayor's Show 136
Lord President of the Council 50 52

MacDonald, Ramsay 66
Macmillan, Maurice 133
Magnus, Sir Philip 29 31 36 59 104

Major, John 155 158
Malaya 85
Malta 85
Manpower Services Commission (MSC)
  133 135 142 146 150
Mansion House, London 12-14 16 96 100
  160
Manual Training 33
Marlborough House 15
Master Bakers and Confectioners 56 71
Masters, Prime Wardens, Upper Bailiff
  of Livery Companies 12 90 95-96 100 138
Mauritius 85
Mechanics' Institute, London 11
Mechanics' Institutes 11
Medals, Silver and Bronze, Institute's 26
  157
Melia, Dr T P 160
Membership of the City and Guilds
  Institute, Diploma of (MCGI) 92 153
Memorandum and Articles of
  Association, Institute's (1880) 21 29
Mercers' Company 14 16 17 20 96
Mercers' Hall 17 20 22 26 32
Ministry of Education 88-90 93-94 99 106-
  107 110
Ministry of Labour 111-112
Ministry of Overseas Development 123-
  124
Moderating Committees, Institute's 72
  82
Morant, Sir Robert 52
Morrison, Peter 136
Multiple-choice Objective Testing 116
  123 128 132
Munro, Air Vice-Marshal Sir David 83

National Advisory Committees,
  Institute's 143 155
National Advisory Council on Education
  for Industry and Commerce 91
National Association for the Promotion
  of Technical Education 34
National Association of British and Irish
  Millers 56 65
National Certificates, Diploma etc 58 65-
  66 78 89 91 95 98-99 108 122 126 141

National Council for Vocational
  Qualifications (NCVQ) 146-147 151 154
  158
National Curriculum 5-16 148
National Examinations Board for
  Agriculture, Horticulture and Allied
  Industries (NEBAHAI) 146
National Joint Industrial Councils 65 71
  76
National Society of Art Masters 80
National Retail Training Council 151
National Vocational Qualifications
  (NVQ) 146-148 150-152 156 158-160
Neal, H Morton 152
Needlemakers' Company 20
New South Wales, Board of Technical
  Education 33 48
New Training Initiative 135
New Zealand 48 85
"Newsom" Report 113
Nicholson, Sir Bryan 158
Northampton Polytechnic (London) 36
  63
Northern Counties Technical
  Examinations Council (NCTEC) 71 75
  110
Nottingham, University College 33

"Open Tech" 135
Operatives 108
Order of St John of Jerusalem 82
Organisation for Rehabilitation through
  Training (ORT) 148
Overseas Work, Institute's 95 120 144-
  145 157 159

Painter-Stainers' Company 14
Palestine 85
Paper Makers' Association 56 71
Parliamentary and Scientific Committee
  94
Part, Sir Anthony 106
Partnership Incorporated 112
Pass (Failure) Rate 32 48 59 61 74 122
Payments on success (Grants to
  Teachers) (1879-92) 23 26 34 46

Pension Schemes, Institute's 74
Percy, Lord Eustace 89-90
Pewterers' Company 20
Pietermaritzberg, South Africa 50
Pitman Examinations Institute (PEI) 145
  156
Plaisterer's Hall 138
Plaisterers' Company 17 20
Plumbers' Company 34
Policy Committee for Education and
  Training, Institute's 121 125 127 133 141
  142
Policy and Practice for Schemes, Institute's
  133 142
Policy on Certificates and Awards,
  Institute's 133 142 152
Polytechnic Institutions, London 36 63
Post Office, The 24 50 65 75
Pothecary, Major W F 83
Potter, F F 83
Practical Competence, Tests of 123 132
Pre-Vocational Education, 14-16 145
Premises, Institute's 46 Britannia Street
  126 139 152
Premises, Institute's, 326 City Road 139
  152
Prentice, Reginald 127
President, Institute's 30 95 109
Prideaux, W T 83 89
Prince Philip Medal 111 157
Prince of Wales, HRH Albert Edward 15
  30-31
Prisoners of War 60 82
Privy Council, H M 105 138 152-153
Prizes 13 19 26 34 59
Professors, Central Institution 19 34
Programme(s) of Technological
  Examinations, Institute's 25 29 30 32 54-
  55 66 73 81 88 106
Psychological Corporation, New York,
  USA 123 128
Public Relations Committee, Institute's
  94 121

Question Papers 27 89

Raising of School-Leaving Age, 1972 129
Regional Advisory Councils 91 98 119
  141 149 157 159
Regional Examining Bodies (Unions) 66
  68-70 73-76 78-79 91 99 107 110-111 119
  124 140 145
Register of Teachers, Institute's 23 27 55
Report of Departmental Committee on
  Examinations for part-time Students
  ("Atholl") 65 70-71 76
Report on Policy in Technical Education 80
Report on the United Nations Conference on
  Science and Technology, Human Resources
  and New Systems of Vocational Training
  and Apprenticeship 112
Report, *Printing and Allied Trades in*
  Scotland 81
Research and Development
  Department, Institute's 132 134 144
Results 89 116
Review of Vocational Qualifications
  (RVQ), Government's 136 145-146
"Robbins" Report 113
Roberts, Sir Owen 16 22
Robotics 146-148
Royal Charters, Institute's, 1900, 1910
  50 58 79 91 105
Royal Family, association with Institute
  31 95
Royal Military College of Science 153
Royal Naval Engineering College 153
Rumbold, Mrs Angela 148

Saddlers' Company 56
Saddlers' Hall 56
Salford, City of 145
St Paul's Cathedral 137
Salters' Company 17 20
Samuel, Viscount 94
Sawyer, Sir William Phillips 16 22
Schofield, Dr Herbert 83
Schools Council 129
Schools Examinations and Assessment
  Council (SEAC) 151
Science and Art Department 12 23-24 26
  30 35 49
Science Museum 137 147

Scottish Consultative Committee,
  Institute's 144
Scottish Education Department 53 144
Scottish Vocational Education Council
  (SCOTVEC) 144-146
Secondary Schools 107 129
Selborne, Earl of (1812-95) 16 20 30 32
Senior Awards, Institute's 133 151 152
  156
Sheffield, Firth College 33
Sheffield University 154
Shelton, William 135
Skill-UK Ltd 150
Skills Testing Service, Institute's 123 132
Skinners' Company 14
Skinners' Hall 95
Society for Diffusion of Useful
  Knowledge 11
Society of Arts, Royal 12 21-22 130 145-
  147
Some Notes on the Educational Activities of
  the Institute 106
South Africa and Rhodesia 85
South Kensington 30 57 97 102
South London Technical Art School,
  City and Guilds (see also City and
  Guilds of London Art School) 22 31 56
  72 76
Standing Committee of Technical
  Examining Bodies 99 107 110
State, The: educational initiatives by 35
  56 115
Stationers' Company 14
Statutes, Institute's 96 105 138 153
Steward, Sir Henry 83 86
Syllabuses 23 29 46 54 66 78 85 89 119 120

Tallow Chandlers' Company 14
Teachers' Certificates 48 98 144
Teachers, Supply of 29 62-63
Teachers, Technical 66 79-80
Technical and Vocational Education
  Initiative (TVEI) 130
Technical Education 11-15 30 56 66 88 99
  104 112
Technical Education in the USA 112
Technical Education, Report 18 22 120

Technical Education, White Paper on, 1956 100
Technical Education for Girls 29 49
Technical Instruction, Royal Commission on (1881-84) 29 32
Technician Education Council (TEC) 59 111 125-128 131 141-142 144 149
Technicians 94 100 103 108-109 118 124-125 135 141 144
Technologists 94 100-101 103
Technology Committee, Institute's 58 65 84 89
Testing Services, City and Guilds 134 136 144
Thatcher, Mrs Margaret 124-125 130
The Further Education of 16-19 Year Olds by Part-time Day Release 127
The Polytechnic, Regent Street, London 74
The Vocational Aspect 107
Times, The 29 50 55 85 89
Tomlinson, George 94
Trade Schools, Local 18 19
Trade Societies, Associations etc. (see also individual bodies) 49 54 56 65 71 77-78
Trades Guild of Learning for the Promotion of Technical and Higher Education among the Working Classes of the United Kingdom 15
Training and Enterprise Councils (TECs) 154 159
Training for the Future 126 132
Training Opportunities Scheme (TOPS) 133
Training Services Agency (TSA) 133 142
Trueman Wood, Sir Henry 18 21
Turners' Company 14

Unified Vocational Preparation (UVP) 134
Union of Educational Institutions (UEI) 71 75 110

Union of Lancashire and Cheshire Institutes (ULCI) 12 50 60 70 75 110
University College, London 22 33
University of Iowa 123
University of London 50 55 151

Vanneck, Sir Peter 136
Vargas Eyre, Dr J 86
Vice-Presidents, Institute's 30
Vintners' Hall 96

Wakefield, City of 145
Wallace, Dr Bill 128
Wallis, H B 84
War, First World 59 61
War, Second World 81-82 88
Warren, H A 109 112
Waterlow, Sir Sydney (1822-1906) 14 16 30 31
Wates, Paul 157
Watney, Sir John 16 22
Welfare State 94 102
Welsh Joint Education Committee (WJEC) 110 159
West Africa 85
West Midlands Regional Advisory Council 98
White, Dr Graham 154
Wilson, Harold 124
Woodbine Parish, Sir David 102 121
Working Men's College 12
Working together: Education and Training, White Paper 146

Yorkshire Council for Further Education (YCFE) 74 98 110
Young, David (Lord Young) 136 148
Youth Opportunities Scheme (YOPS) 134-135
Youth Training Scheme (YTS) 135 146 148
YTS Certification Board 146 148